Praise for *The Definitive Guide to Instructional Coaching*

There simply isn't a bigger influence than Jim Knight in the world of instructional coaching. His words, through workshops, keynotes, books, blogs, and articles, give us a greater understanding of how to coach and learn from those we coach. I always look forward to his next piece of research, and this book is a compilation of his greatest hits from the last couple of decades, and a guide to doing that work to a deeper degree. I am fortunate to call Jim a mentor and a friend, and I see this deeply impactful book as a go-to resource for a very long time.

—*Peter DeWitt, EdD, leadership coach, author, and* Education Week *blogger*

Based on his own experiences, significant research, and the current pulse of the profession, Jim Knight has assembled sets of strategies, principles, processes, and techniques for anyone who prepares, guides, or coaches teachers. Looking closely, one also discovers an even richer vein of information about the art of instructional excellence. On the matter of coaching feedback, for example, Knight provides stunningly sophisticated descriptions of what good teachers attend to. This well-organized book by one of the nation's leading authorities on the coaching process should live on the shelves of every principal, staff developer, and mentor teacher. Experienced instructional coaches and aspiring coaches alike will benefit from this accessible handbook.

—*Robert J. Garmston, EdD, and Arthur L. Costa, EdD,*
Professors Emeriti, California State University, Sacramento, and coauthors of
Cognitive Coaching: Developing Self-Directed Leaders and Learners

Just when I thought my coaching tool kit was complete, Jim Knight writes a must-have for every coach, coach of coaches, and leader of instructional teams. *The Definitive Guide to Instructional Coaching* is packed with the essentials for creating and implementing a coaching culture that will improve instruction, communication, and even your personal life. I am a better person and coach because I believe and practice the Partnership Principles in every area of my life. Learning to be a better listener and questioner improved my communication with both colleagues and family. The closing sections of each chapter are my favorite because they demand change, growth, and action—all while holding true to the spirit of the Partnership Principles.

—*Keysha McIntyre, educational consultant, MoldingMinds Moments, LLC*

Who better to write the definitive guide to instructional coaching than Dr. Jim Knight—the guy who coined the term *instructional coaching*? This guide provides a comprehensive exploration of instructional coaching and what helps it deliver great results for students. I particularly liked the section on system support. Great work by individual coaches and teachers will have so much more impact when the system is aligned and supportive. Administrators and coaches will frequently turn to Knight's practical advice as they take steps down the implementation pathway.

—*John Campbell, Founding Director, Growth Coaching International*

Jim Knight's books, articles, presentations, and one-on-one conversations have strengthened my skills and understanding of coaching from my earliest days as a promoter of coaching in schools. For readers with substantial experience in coaching, *The Definitive Guide to Instructional Coaching* will provide reinforcement, reminders, and continued opportunities for growth. Those who are newer to the coaching field will find direction for their next steps. "All educators deserve coaching." Jim's work supports all of us who want to make that happen.

—*Stephen Barkley, author of* Instructional Coaching with the End in Mind

The Definitive Guide to Instructional Coaching nails it. Everything an instructional coach needs to know is in this book. All the steps and components are spelled out and crystal clear. Our Educational Coaching Network and graduate coaching courses will be using this book as our primary instructional coaching resource.

—*Alison Gordon, EdD, coordinator, Educational Coaching Network,*
School of Education & Social Policy, Northwestern University

Jim's work has been paramount to my professional career. Five years ago, I began my career as an instructional coach and quickly began acquiring Jim's books. First, I learned about the Partnership Principles and how vital they are to establishing a strong teacher-coach relationship. These principles really help you understand how humanistic the profession is, and without their presence a strong relationship built on trust is not guaranteed. Next, the Impact Cycle really helps break down the coaching cycle into a simple, easily understood framework. This certainly isn't to say that coaching is easy, but Jim's framework helps coaches understand the process in a way that isn't so overwhelming. Finally, 2021–2022 will be my first as a building principal. Jim's work hasn't just helped me understand how important coaches are to the field of education, but I have also realized how important it is to lead and support a staff from a coaching mindset.

—*Heath Hesse, elementary principal, Stormont, Iowa*

THE DEFINITIVE GUIDE TO

INSTRUCTIONAL COACHING

Also by Jim Knight

*Evaluating Instructional Coaching:
People, Programs, and Partnership*
with Sharon Thomas, Ann Hoffman, and Michelle Harris

*The Instructional Playbook:
The Missing Link for Translating Research into Practice*
with Ann Hoffman, Michelle Harris, and Sharon Thomas

THE DEFINITIVE GUIDE TO

INSTRUCTIONAL
COACHING

SEVEN
FACTORS
FOR
SUCCESS

JIM
KNIGHT

ascd

Alexandria, Virginia USA

1703 N. Beauregard St. • Alexandria, VA 22311-1714 USA
Phone: 800-933-2723 or 703-578-9600 • Fax: 703-575-5400
Website: www.ascd.org • Email: member@ascd.org
Author guidelines: www.ascd.org/write

Ranjit Sidhu, *CEO & Executive Director;* Penny Reinart, *Chief Impact Officer;* Genny Ostertag, *Senior Director, Content Acquisitions and Editing;* Susan Hills, *Senior Acquisitions Editor;* Julie Houtz, *Director, Book Editing;* Miriam Calderone, *Editor;* Thomas Lytle, *Creative Director;* Donald Ely, *Art Director;* Georgia Park, *Senior Graphic Designer;* Valerie Younkin, *Senior Production Designer;* Kelly Marshall, *Production Manager;* Shajuan Martin, *E-Publishing Specialist*

Cover Design by Chase Christensen.

All web links in this book are correct as of the publication date below but may have become inactive or otherwise modified since that time. If you notice a deactivated or changed link, please email books@ascd.org with the words "Link Update" in the subject line. In your message, please specify the web link, the book title, and the page number on which the link appears.

PAPERBACK ISBN: 978-1-4166-3066-1   ASCD product #121006

PDF E-BOOK ISBN: 978-1-4166-3067-8; see Books in Print for other formats.

Quantity discounts are available: email programteam@ascd.org or call 800-933-2723, ext. 5773, or 703-575-5773. For desk copies, go to www.ascd.org/deskcopy.

ASCD Member Book No. FY22-2 (Nov. 2021 PSI+). ASCD Member Books mail to Premium (P), Select (S), and Institutional Plus (I+) members on this schedule: Jan, PSI+; Feb, P; Apr, PSI+; May, P; Jul, PSI+; Aug, P; Sep, PSI+; Nov, PSI+; Dec, P. For current details on membership, see www.ascd.org/membership.

Library of Congress Cataloging-in-Publication Data
Names: Knight, Jim, author.
Title: The definitive guide to instructional coaching : seven factors for success / Jim Knight.
Description: Alexandria, VA : ASCD, 2022. | Includes bibliographical references and index.
Identifiers: LCCN 2021031580 (print) | LCCN 2021031581 (ebook) | ISBN 9781416630661
    (paperback) | ISBN 9781416630678 (pdf)
Subjects: LCSH: Mentoring in education. | Teachers--Professional relationships.
Classification: LCC LB1731.4 .K63 2022 (print) | LCC LB1731.4 (ebook) | DDC 371.102--dc23
LC record available at https://lccn.loc.gov/2021031580
LC ebook record available at https://lccn.loc.gov/2021031581

30 29 28 27 26 25 24 23 22   1 2 3 4 5 6 7 8 9 10 11 12

This book is dedicated to Ben Knight—not only the official Rock, Paper, Scissors champion of Lawrence, Kansas, but also a gifted and creative musician and sound technician.

Ben, I'm very grateful for the way you make sure our videos and institutes sound and look perfect, but even more, I am moved by your kindness, compassion, and determination to live with integrity and do the right thing. I'm very proud to call you my son.

THE DEFINITIVE GUIDE TO

INSTRUCTIONAL COACHING
SEVEN FACTORS FOR SUCCESS

Preface

There is a degree of hubris, I admit, in choosing to call this book *The Definitive Guide to Instructional Coaching.* But that title has served as the northern point on a compass, guiding me as I write. I have tried to create a document that lives up to it, providing a concise yet comprehensive review of the beliefs, processes, knowledge, and skills that instructional coaches can use to guide their practice and administrators can employ to create a coaching program that has an unmistakably positive impact on students.

Coaching is essential for the kind of growth we need to see in schools. Real learning occurs in real life, when people work hard to solve real-life challenges. Workshops, books, and webinars can provide us with an overview of ideas, but we only adopt and internalize these ideas when we apply them to our professional practice. That kind of real-life learning requires goals that matter deeply to us and to our students, both because they are based on a clear understanding of reality and because we have chosen them for ourselves.

Coaches help with each aspect of this kind of learning by partnering with teachers to (1) establish a clear picture of reality; (2) set emotionally compelling, student-focused goals; and (3) learn, adapt, and integrate teaching practices that help teachers and students hit goals. That kind of comprehensive learning is next to impossible for busy educators to achieve without a coach.

Coaching done well is an excellent investment in children's lives. Successful coaches need to be experts at instruction while at the same time honoring the expertise of the professionals with whom they collaborate. They need to understand the complexities of personal change and communicate in ways that provide the support others need to change. Coaches need to lead, listen, and partner with teachers to move through a coaching process. They also need to work in settings that are organized to give them the best chance to succeed.

I address all these ideas and more in my discussion of the Success Factors that are the focus of this book. These factors are the product of more than 25 years of research on instructional coaching. I have summarized that research, conducted first at the University of Kansas Center for Research on Learning and now at the Instructional Coaching Group (ICG), in many books—including *Coaching Classroom Management* (2006), *Instructional Coaching* (2007), *Unmistakable Impact* (2011), *High-Impact Instruction* (2013), *Focus on Teaching* (2014), *Better Conversations* (2016), *The Impact Cycle* (2017), and *The Instructional Playbook* (2020)—and in many journal articles.

This book collects the most vital ideas from all those publications in one volume. More important, however, it is intended to describe what we have learned about coaching since those materials were published. Over the years, my colleagues and I at ICG have interviewed hundreds of educators from across the world. I have also had the good fortune to work directly with many excellent coaches in various research studies I have led in Lawrence and Topeka, Kansas; Beaverton, Oregon; and Othello, Washington. Many of the strategies and skills you will read about here were developed by people who dedicate each day to having an unmistakably positive impact on students.

This book also summarizes the work of researchers and authors who have influenced the way I understand change, conversations, psychology, instruction, organizational development, learning communities, and so forth. This research places coaching in the broader context of recent insights into professional learning.

Perhaps most important, this book documents the many mistakes we have made and what we've learned from those mistakes as we've developed our understanding of instructional coaching. If you were to read everything I've ever written in order of publication, you would undeniably read a chronicle of mistakes and lessons learned. I share mistakes encountered along the way here so that you can avoid making them in your practice. As Eleanor Roosevelt famously said, "Learn from the mistakes of others. You can't live long enough to make them all yourself." In that spirit, I hope this guide helps you to make your own mistakes and learn your own lessons. Let's keep the learning going, because when we learn, so do our students.

Acknowledgments

I used to skip the acknowledgments in books the way people skip through credits at the end of a movie. But having written a few books myself now, I know just how important all those names are. The acknowledgments are like a family tree for a book: each person's ideas, actions, or words of encouragement spurred the author on, and each book is really the realization of the work of many other people. That is especially true of this book, which brings together a lot of the work I have done over more than two decades studying instructional coaching. I am profoundly grateful to all the people listed here and many more.

To my life partner, Jenny: How lucky can one man get to have a partner as loving, supportive, smart, and forgiving as you? Thank you for showing me the beautiful things in the world. This book, like so much of my life, has only been possible because your unwavering support has helped me write every word I put down on every page.

To my children, most of you grown up and making the world a better place each day: You inspire me, encourage me, and make me want to be a better person. Geoff, Cam, Dave, Emily, Ben, Isaiah, and Luke, I love you and am grateful for your patience with me as I do my best to make my way forward. I love watching you, as Maya Angelou once wrote, "astonish a mean world with your acts of kindness."

To my colleagues at the Instructional Coaching Group, Ann Hoffman, Brooke Deaton, Chase Christensen, Emily Malatesta, Erin Krownapple, Geoff Knight, Jenny Ryschon Knight, Matt Kelly, Michelle Harris, Ruth Ryschon, and Sharon Thomas: How fortunate we all are to get to work with one another. I am grateful for your gifts and your dedication to and support of one another, but I am especially grateful for your commitment to our goal of excellent instruction, every day, in every class, for every student, everywhere. Together, we really are making it happen.

To my editors, Susan Hills and Kirsten McBride: Susan, thank you for your ongoing support of this project. Your patient enthusiasm has gotten me going many, many times, and I'm grateful to be welcomed as part of the team at ASCD. Kirsten, thank you for your longtime dedication to my work. My guess is that over the two decades we've worked together, you have edited more than 95 percent of the words I've put into print. I've yet to write a page that you haven't been able to improve, and I can't begin to calculate how important you have been to any success I've experienced.

To the researchers and writers who have shaped my thinking: I have tried to acknowledge my debt to all of you in the Going Deeper sections of my books. I am especially grateful to John Campbell and Christian van Nieuwerburgh for all you have taught me, and especially for your friendship. And while it is impossible to thank everyone who has influenced or supported me in some way, I have made an attempt through ICG's annual Don Deshler Leadership Award, which goes to people whose ideas and support are so important that the group's work would not exist without them. Past winners include Don Deshler, Jean Schumaker, Joellen Killion, Michael Fullan, Randy Sprick, Ann Hoffman, Dan Alpert, Doris Williams, and Parker Palmer.

To educators: Over the years I have interviewed hundreds of coaches, teachers, and administrators whose ideas have become central to our work. I'm especially grateful to the coaches and teachers with whom I've partnered in Topeka and Lawrence, Kansas; Beaverton, Oregon; and Othello, Washington, as well as to the many educators who agreed to be interviewed for this book. Thank you for your willingness to teach me, and thank you even more for your dedication to children.

To musical artists: I listened to a lot of music while writing this book, starting with Mitsuko Uchida's recordings of Mozart's piano sonatas and Zhu Xiao Mai's recordings of Bach's best-known piano compositions. I remain a huge fan of the Prestige recordings of Miles Davis and John Coltrane (both separate and together). Additionally, I wrote a lot to Ludovico Einaudi's *Seven Days Walking* after Peter DeWitt recommended Einaudi to me. Most recently, following the advice of my neoclassical music coach Heath Hesse,

I've been obsessed with the music of Ólafur Arnalds, Nils Frahm, Jóhann Jóhannsson, and especially Max Richter, whose *Sleep* recordings, at more than eight hours long, have been the soundtrack to many days spent writing.

My sincere thanks also go to the following educators whose comments were used in the book:

- Dr. Alison Gordon, Instructor, Master of Science in Education Program Coordinator, Educational Coaching Network, School of Education & Social Policy, Northwestern University
- Amber Theinel, Instructional Math Coach, Freedom Middle School, Franklin, Tennessee
- Angela Adams, Lead Coach, Carolina Teacher Induction Program, College of Education, University of South Carolina
- Angela Kolb, Special Education Teacher, Warner Elementary, Spring Arbor, Michigan
- April Strong, Instructional Coach, Martin County Schools, Stuart, Florida
- Dr. Cameron Muir, Associate Principal—Curriculum and Instruction, Glenbrook South High School, Glenview, Illinois
- Kevin A. Heron, Instructional Coach, Deer Park Elementary School, Newport News, Virginia
- Keysha McIntyre, Math Lead Specialist, Fulton County Schools, Atlanta, Georgia
- Leigh Anstadt, Coach of Coaches, Canyons School District, Sandy, Utah
- Dr. Mark Dowley, Director of Staff Development and Instruction, Crowther Centre, Brighton Grammar School, Victoria, Australia
- Megan Greene, Elementary Technology Integration Coach, Franklin Community Schools, Franklin, Indiana
- Rachel LeForce, Instructional Coach, Smith Elementary, Frisco, Texas
- Sharon Sheehan, Coordinator, Educational Coaching Network, School of Education & Social Policy, Northwestern University

Seven Success Factors for Instructional Coaching

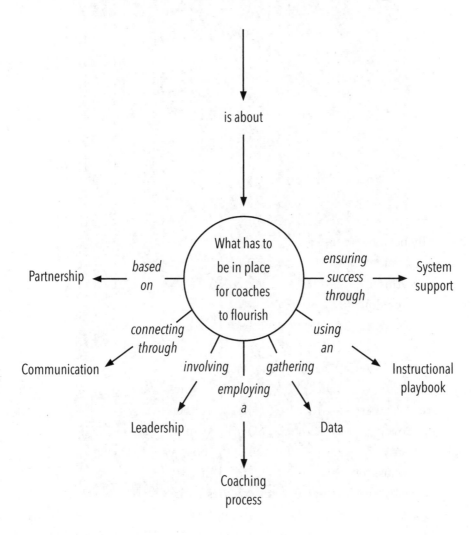

Introduction

Coaching done well may be the most effective
intervention designed for human performance.

—Atul Gawande, *Personal Best*

Megan Greene will never forget her first week as a K–6 instructional coach in Franklin, Indiana. As she watched all her colleagues get ready for their classes, she sat at her desk not knowing what to do. She missed being in the classroom, feeling at home with her students and doing what she thought she did best in the world.

When Megan was in high school, she didn't really know what she wanted to do for a living. She had good grades, played sports, and had friends, but, in her words, she "was nothing to write home about." In the end, she decided to attend Ball State University, famous for its educational program, and study to become a teacher.

Something clicked when Megan started her studies. "I was no rock star," Megan says, "but when I stepped into the classroom, I knew that the passion was there, and I had such a strong desire to grow as a professional." When she finally became a teacher, Megan felt for the first time that she was doing something well: "My work and students brought joy to me that didn't compare to anything else," she says. For 15 years, Megan's classroom felt like home, and she flourished.

When a job posting came up for an instructional coaching position in Megan's school district, her coworkers told her it was the perfect fit, but she decided that she couldn't give up the classroom. Then two new positions were posted for instructional technology coaches, which seemed an even better fit for Megan—after all, she loved to learn, loved technology, and loved the idea of helping teachers use technology effectively in the classroom. This time she couldn't resist, so she applied for one of the positions and was hired. After 15 years in the classroom, she was going to be an instructional coach.

Administrators knew that their coaches and principals would need professional development for their coaching to be effective, so they asked all coaches and principals in the district to attend the Instructional Coaching Group's five-day Intensive Instructional Coaching Institute in Lawrence,

Kansas. (We—and when I say "we" in this book, I'm referring to my ICG colleagues and myself—don't use the term *intensive* lightly here; the institute addresses much of the content in this book.)

While Megan was grateful for her administrators' support, she still wasn't sure she'd made the right decision. She loved the chance to be with her colleagues and appreciated the content and activities the institute offered, but at the end of the day, she felt lost. Sometimes, after putting on a brave face during the workshop, she would go up to her room feeling so confused and sad that she would burst into tears.

Not long after returning from the workshop, Megan told her husband she was seriously considering quitting her coaching job because she really wasn't sure she could succeed. He reminded her that she had always found a way to move forward before. That night, Megan made up her mind: No matter what, she wasn't going to quit. She would give coaching her best.

Back at school, Megan started by going into classrooms and asking teachers how she could help, explaining that they would be helping her by letting her help them. She also sought out the support of other coaches in her district who were experiencing doubts and insecurities about coaching similar to hers. Bit by bit, teachers became more comfortable in their coaching roles. Megan soon found teachers who were willing to move through the Impact Cycle (see Chapter 4), and she started to implement many of the ideas she'd learned at the institute. "Ultimately, coaching changed my life and literally hundreds of other lives in just one school year," she says.

The results clearly show that Megan was a successful coach. She completed 46 deep coaching cycles, with 100 percent of participating teachers expressing interest in completing another cycle and saying they would recommend coaching to colleagues. Four veteran teachers with over 35 years' experience each completed a cycle. A total of 556 elementary students and 2,630 secondary students were affected. At the end of the year, Megan wrote us to describe how she felt about being a coach: "I could not be more thankful for the people who believed in me when I didn't believe in myself. I'm no longer lost—I'm reborn!"

Like Megan, thousands of educators go from teaching to coaching only to find themselves doubting their decision. Unfortunately, as we will see in future chapters, not all stories end as happily as Megan's. When coaches don't receive support or learn and practice the knowledge and skills they need, they often aren't successful. Coaching is a completely new position for most people, so they need guidance if they are to have the impact they dream of having.

All instructional coaches need a tool to help them know where to start and what to do, and it is my hope that this book can be that tool. I wrote this book to summarize what I have learned over more than 20 years studying instructional coaching and in my ongoing work with over 150,000 instructional coaches on six different continents. (You can read a summary of my findings at www.instructionalcoaching.com/research.) I've organized what I've learned into seven Success Factors that every coach, coaching director, and administrator should understand and be able to apply to create a powerful coaching program (see below). These factors are essential not only for coaching to be effective, but for any change initiative to succeed.

1. The Partnership Principles
2. Communication skills
3. Coaches as leaders
4. The Impact Cycle
5. Data
6. The instructional playbook
7. System support

This book is divided into three sections: Who You Are, What You Do, and Where You Work.

Who You Are
Factor One: The Partnership Principles

In Chapter 1, I explain that the way coaches interact with others frequently determines whether their coaching is successful. If coaches see themselves as superior to others, they may find that others are not interested in hearing what they have to say. As Massachusetts Institute of Technology organizational development specialist Edgar Schein (2009, 2013; Schein & Schein, 2018) has explained, people often resist ideas shared with them if they perceive that the status they think they deserve is not being acknowledged.

Carl Rogers first popularized the phrase "way of being" in his 1980 book of the same name. Put simply, "way of being" refers to how we are in the world with others, including whichever set of principles we live by. (And whether we realize it or not, every one of us lives according to a set of principles.) The following seven Partnership Principles (described at greater length in Chapter 1) form one such set that can serve as a foundation for mutually humanizing learning conversations:

1. **Equality:** I believe that everyone has the same worth. No individual or group is more valuable than any other.
2. **Choice:** I recognize that I will only get commitment from others when I honor their autonomy. As Tim Gallwey says, "When you insist, I resist" (2000, p. 14).
3. **Voice:** I act in ways that make it easy for my conversation partners to share their ideas, thoughts, and emotions because I want to know what they have to say.
4. **Reflection:** I understand coaching as a meeting of the minds that can involve (a) looking *back,* to consider how something did or didn't work; (b) looking *at,* to consider how things are going; or (c) looking *ahead,* by using what I know to make future improvements (Knight, 2011).
5. **Dialogue:** I ensure that my coaching partners' ideas can shape my thinking as much as or more than my ideas shape theirs. This means I let go of the *need* to be right so that I can *do* what is right.
6. **Praxis:** I understand that we learn best when we apply ideas to our day-to-day experiences. Learning happens best through action.
7. **Reciprocity:** I go into every conversation expecting to learn from my conversation partner. As Robert Half is often said to have stated, "When one teaches, two learn."

Factor Two: Communication Skills

Coaching is, above all, a conversation or series of conversations focused on professional growth. For this reason, coaches need to understand both the nature of the teacher's personal experience of change and the communication habits and skills that make talking about change possible.

As I explain in Chapter 2, all change is self-change, and coaches are more successful when they stop trying to motivate others and start trying to create the conditions in which others can recognize and realize their own immense potential. Done well, coaching fosters hope and empowers others to motivate themselves. Such coaching requires what Christian van Nieuwerburgh (2017) calls "managed conversation[s]" (p. 5). Three skills are especially important for these conversations: *listening, questioning,* and *balancing telling with asking.*

Factor Three: Coaches as Leaders

The difference between coaches who have a positive impact and those who do not comes down to leadership. In Chapter 3, I describe what leadership looks like for successful coaches and what coaches can do to become powerful forces for good in their schools. Leadership is more complex than we might think, especially for coaches who engage in equal-status, peer-to-peer conversations with others. Leadership among peers in complex organizations involves much more than a persuasively delivered call to action.

I divide leadership into two parts: *leading ourselves* and *leading others.* To lead ourselves, we need to know our purpose and principles, how to use our time effectively, how to take care of ourselves, and how to develop habits that enable us to do these things. To lead others, we need to make good decisions, interact with others in ways that expand our capacities, foster deep knowledge and deep implementation, and create alignment with others.

Often we think of leaders as almost superhuman. These heroes—Dr. Martin Luther King, Abraham Lincoln, Mahatma Gandhi, Mother Theresa, and others—seem like saints who have accomplished so much that we could never approach achieving similar results. And yet their fights—for freedom, health, equality, respect, goodness—are fights all of us can join. When a coach's kindness and empathy help a teacher find self-efficacy, when a teacher's high expectations compel a student to believe she can be more than she realizes, when a coach's commitment to self-improvement helps him better coach teachers so that students improve—in all these cases, coaches and teachers are engaged in the same struggle as our saintly heroes: the fight to make the world a better place. To lead with the Partnership Principles in mind is to hold up hope that the world can and will be better.

What You Do
Factor Four: The Impact Cycle

The Partnership Principles suggest a way of being for coaches, but coaches also need a structure for coaching conversations. The Impact Cycle, a deceptively simple instructional coaching cycle, is one such structure and the focus of Chapter 4 in this book. There are three stages to the Impact Cycle—Identify, Learn, and Improve (see Figure I.1):

1. **Identify:** Coaches partner with teachers to identify a clear picture of reality; a powerful, emotionally compelling, easy, reachable, and student-focused (or PEERS) goal; and a strategy the teacher will implement to try meeting that goal.
2. **Learn:** The coach describes the strategy to be implemented, often with the help of a checklist, and shows the teacher one or more models of the strategy to ensure that the teacher is comfortable with it.
3. **Improve:** The coach partners with the teacher to make adaptations until the PEERS goal identified in the first stage is met.

Factor Five: Data

My friend John Campbell, one of the leading coaching pioneers in Australia, is responsible for one of my favorite quotes about coaching: "If there's no goal, it is just a nice conversation."[1] If John is correct, and I believe he is, then data, which I describe in Chapter 5, are essential. They help us to paint a clear picture of our destination and reveal whether we are on or off track. I suggest that data be gathered for two main foci for coaching—engagement and achievement:

---

[1]When I asked John about this quotation, he was quick to tell me he first heard it from coaching expert Tony Grant.

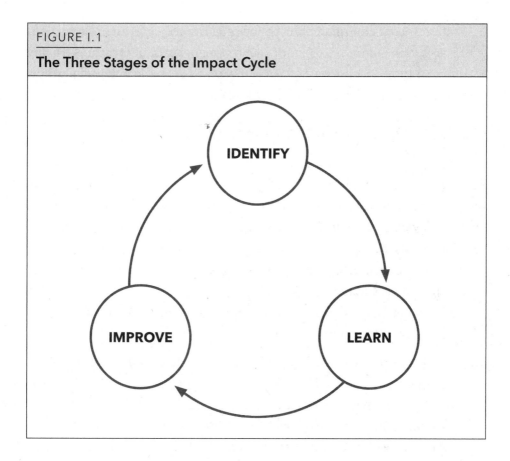

FIGURE I.1

The Three Stages of the Impact Cycle

1. **Engagement:** Data can be gathered on at least three kinds of engagement: behavioral, cognitive, and emotional. *Behavioral engagement* measures whether students are doing what they are supposed to be doing—that is, whether they are on task. *Cognitive engagement* measures whether students are experiencing the learning their teacher intends for them to experience from an activity. Finally, *emotional engagement* measures the extent to which students feel they belong in their school, are physically and psychologically safe, engage in positive and meaningful experiences at school, have friends, and have hope.

2. **Achievement:** To measure achievement, teachers must first identify what students need to learn during a unit or a lesson and then use different kinds of assessments (e.g., selected-response or short-answer

tests, checks for understanding, rubrics). Sometimes an informal conversation is enough to identify achievement goals, but teachers usually need more precise methods of gathering data to make the adaptations necessary for students to meet those goals.

Factor Six: The Instructional Playbook

Goals are essential, but they don't mean much without a pathway to reach them. For this reason, instructional coaches must have a deep knowledge of high-impact teaching strategies. Coaches partner with teachers to identify, explain, model, and adapt teaching strategies so teachers and their students can meet goals. These high-impact strategies are often organized, summarized, and described in what I call an "instructional playbook" (described at greater length in Chapter 6).

In my opinion, every instructional coach needs to have an instructional playbook consisting of three sections:

1. A short list of the high-impact teaching strategies that coaches most frequently use with teachers
2. A set of one-page documents summarizing the purpose, research, and essential information for each teaching strategy
3. Checklists for the strategies that coaches share with teachers

The playbook is a living document that should be used to organize learning about teaching strategies. Coaches should revisit all aspects of the playbook frequently, revising the contents as they identify new and better strategies.

Where You Work
Factor Seven: System Support

When coaches flourish, it is often because they work in settings where leaders are intentional and disciplined about providing the support necessary for coaching success. Without such support, coaches often struggle to have any impact at all. In Chapter 7, I describe what a supportive coaching system entails.

Districts that support coaches ensure that everyone involved understands what coaching is and why it is necessary to address the complexities of the stages of implementation. They also hire great coaches, clarify their roles and how they are to use their time, and explain what is and is not confidential during coaching. Successful districts also create structures and cultures that promote learning. Finally, in settings where coaches are most effective, principals explicitly support coaches and, in fact, are often coaches themselves.

Final Sections of Each Chapter

Each chapter of this book concludes with four sections:

1. **To Sum Up:** A quick summary of the main ideas in the chapter.
2. **Reflection Questions:** Questions for self-reflection or group discussion about the chapter.
3. **Going Deeper:** Suggestions for additional resources to extend learning about the ideas in the chapter.
4. **What's Next?:** Some quick suggestions for how to start implementing the ideas in the chapter.

To Sum Up

The following seven factors must be in place for instructional coaching programs to flourish:

1. A coaching way of being grounded in the seven Partnership Principles of *equality, choice, voice, reflection, dialogue, praxis,* and *reciprocity.*
2. Using effective communication habits and skills to ensure that teachers experience productive coaching that leads to powerful, positive changes for student learning and well-being.
3. Leadership, which involves coaches leading both themselves and others.
4. An effective coaching process such as the Impact Cycle, which moves through three stages: Identify (develop a clear picture of reality, a goal, and a strategy to be implemented to reach the goal), Learn (provide clear explanations that often involve checklists and modeling), and Improve (make adaptations until the goal is met).

5. Gathering and analyzing engagement or achievement data with teachers so that they can set goals and monitor progress.

6. Ensuring that coaches have a deep knowledge of the instructional practices they share, possibly by creating an instructional playbook.

7. System support, meaning everyone in the system works together to support the coaching process so that teachers can learn and grow and students can excel.

Reflection Questions

1. Should you work from the Partnership Principles? If so, do you or does anything else need to change? If not, what principles *should* drive your actions? Is anything keeping you from working from the Partnership Principles?

2. How important is communication for a fulfilling life? What is one step you can take toward becoming the communicator you want to be?

3. What is one thing you can do today to improve as a leader? Why is this important? Are you going to do it?

4. What needs to be in place for you to learn and implement the Impact Cycle?

5. What data do you gather? How reliable are these data? Do you need to expand the kinds of data you collect? Do you need to change anything about the way you collect data?

6. Do you have an instructional playbook? If not, do you think you should? How deep is your understanding of the teaching strategies you share?

7. How might the administrators in your school and district better support coaches?

Going Deeper

Since the seven Success Factors discussed in this book are largely the culmination of the research and analysis my colleagues and I have conducted during the last two decades, I hope readers will forgive me for mentioning some of my own books here. (In future chapters, many helpful books by authors other than myself make up the bulk of the Going Deeper recommendations.)

- *The Impact Cycle: What Instructional Coaches Should Do to Foster Powerful Improvements in Teaching* (2018) is the most complete treatment available of the Impact Cycle at the heart of instructional coaching. The book contains detailed chapters about each stage of the cycle and dozens of resources that coaches can use.
- *Better Conversations: Coaching Ourselves and Each Other to Be More Credible, Caring, and Connected* (2016) provides readers with an overview of useful conversation beliefs and habits for coaches. Since conversation is what coaches engage in the most, I think this book is essential, but I also hope that it will inspire coaches to communicate in ways that are more respectful, affirming, and loving.
- *High-Impact Instruction: A Framework for Great Teaching* (2013) is my most complete discussion of effective instructional practices organized around four areas: content planning, formative assessment, instruction, and community building.
- *The Instructional Playbook* (2020), which I cowrote with Ann Hoffman, Michelle Harris, and Sharon Thomas, provides the tools people need to create an instructional playbook.
- *Focus on Teaching: Using Video for High-Impact Instruction* (2014) explains why video is essential to effective professional development and how any professional developer can help teachers use video to improve their practice.

What's Next?

When coaches first start to learn about the seven Success Factors, they may be overwhelmed by all the books, materials, and other information they encounter. Not surprisingly, they often ask a simple question: "Where should I start?" I believe coaches need to start by developing a deep understanding of the beliefs at the heart of instructional coaching: the Partnership Principles, which are the focus of the next chapter.

You can find additional materials to support your practice at www.instructionalcoaching.com/bookstore/ the-definitive-guide-to-instructional-coaching.

In addition, I have written a reflection guide designed to enhance and extend your understanding and application of the ideas and strategies in this book. Find it at www.instructionalcoaching.com/bookstore.

Who You Are

Learning Map for Chapter 1

The Partnership Principles

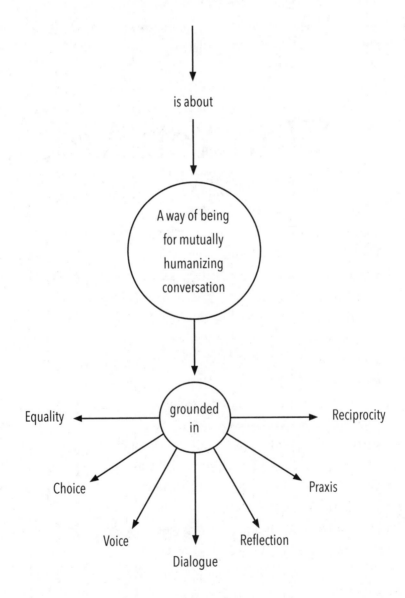

is about

A way of being for mutually humanizing conversation

grounded in

Equality

Reciprocity

Choice

Praxis

Voice

Reflection

Dialogue

1 The Partnership Principles

When [people] cannot choose, [they] cease to be [people].
—Anthony Burgess

Chandra Edwards was an accomplished, award-winning teacher who chose to become an instructional coach so she could have a bigger impact on students' lives. "If I work with all the teachers in the school," she reasoned, "I can make a difference for a lot of kids."

Chandra didn't receive much professional development on how to be a coach, but she felt she knew quite a bit about effective instruction. She'd gone to workshops based on Marzano's and Hattie's work and even felt a bit nerdy on the subject, since she actually *enjoyed* reading their research summaries. In her classroom, she used cooperative learning structures like Mix-Pair-Share and Numbered Heads Together, as well as learning maps from my own book *High-Impact Instruction* (Knight, 2013). She had also attended a lot of training based on Charlotte Danielson's book *Enhancing Professional Practice* (2007), which her district used to evaluate teachers. Looking ahead to her first year as an instructional coach, she was excited to share what she knew.

Once she got started, however, Chandra was surprised to discover that teachers weren't all that keen to work with her despite all she had to share. She knew teachers were busy—after all, she'd been in the classroom for 18 years herself—so she decided to focus on relationship building with a few of her closest work colleagues. When she asked them if they'd do her a big favor and work with her, they gladly agreed because they liked Chandra.

Chandra was kind of relieved that she was able to ease into coaching. She wasn't sure what she should do once she had people willing to work with her. But she had been a successful teacher, and she assumed coaching would be a similar process. Since she knew about the power of feedback, she decided to observe teachers, share her observations about what seemed to be working well in their classrooms, and possibly suggest one or two areas for improvement. In other words, she'd share "a glow and grow" with every teacher she observed and then maybe talk about strategies they could use to grow their practice further.

Right away, Chandra realized the conversations she was having didn't feel right. For one, she was doing most of the talking, which she knew wasn't the way to coach. But most troubling was the fact that these teachers, who had gone out of their way to support her, didn't seem to want to hear what she had to say. "It feels like they're looking right through me when I talk," she told a friend.

From there, things got worse. Her friends thanked her for her time, but they didn't implement her suggestions and said they didn't have time to work with her anymore. At the same time, Chandra's principal expected to see results and wanted her to work with some teachers who were really struggling. "Those teachers need to get better quickly," the principal told her, "because they are letting down their students and the school with their ineffective teaching."

The principal was right to say the teachers were struggling. The classes Chandra observed were boring and confusing. But how could she help the teachers if they didn't want to work with her? Sometimes they wouldn't even look her in the eye when she gave them feedback. Chandra came to hate having these conversations, yet she also felt pressure to show results. Her position was grant-funded, and when the grant was gone, her job would be gone, too, if she didn't clearly show that she was making an impact.

In an effort to turn things around, Chandra asked her principal to make teachers attend workshops she was holding before school every other Wednesday. But these compulsory workshops turned out to be agony for both the teachers and Chandra. The teachers made it clear that they didn't want to be there, and their comments during sessions all seemed to be about why the strategies wouldn't work. Chandra pushed harder, explaining why everyone should do what she was saying, and the teachers pushed back. "Why are these teachers so resistant?" she kept asking herself.

Chandra tried other techniques. She created a weekly email for teachers about effective teaching practices. She conducted walkthroughs of teachers' classrooms, leaving observation notes in teachers' mailboxes. She sat in on meetings of professional learning communities (PLCs). Soon she began to suspect that the teachers didn't like her—and worse still, that she was having no lasting impact on instruction and student learning in her school.

Though Chandra Edwards is fictional, the anecdote above reflects comments I have heard from dozens of instructional coaches about their experiences working with teachers. People go into coaching with enthusiasm, eager but unprepared for the realities of their new role, and then are surprised to find that teachers are less than excited about working with them. If coaches then become more direct in their approach, teachers become even less interested, and eventually the coaches give up.

Teachers like the ones in Chandra's school aren't resisting ideas but, rather, poorly designed professional development. The problem doesn't lie with them, but with underprepared coaches who treat their teachers the way they treat students. Thankfully, by learning about the seven Partnership Principles that are the focus of this chapter, coaches can help ensure that teachers welcome rather than resist the coaching process.

The Partnership Principles are probably the most impactful of all the coaching ideas I've shared over time. I created them by synthesizing theories from education, business, psychology, sociology, cultural anthropology, and philosophy of science—in particular, the works of Richard Bernstein (1983), Peter Block (1993), David Bohm (1996), Riane Eisler (1987), Paulo Freire (1970), and Peter Senge (1990).

I've written about the principles in several other publications, including *Partnership Learning Fieldbook* (2002), *Instructional Coaching* (2007), *Unmistakable Impact* (2011), and *The Impact Cycle* (2018), and I've summarized them in many articles and books. The truth is, I've written about the principles so much that I can't blame you if you thought, "What? The principles again?" when you saw what this chapter was about. But our conception of the principles has been transformed in recent years by both ICG's own research and new insights gained from the literature. In this chapter, then, I describe a new way of understanding the principles.

What Is a Principle?

The *Oxford English Dictionary* defines a *principle* as a "fundamental source from which something proceeds... the ultimate basis upon which the existence of something depends" (Oxford University Press, 1981, p. 2303). In other words, principles guide our actions whether we are conscious of them or not. For example, a person who lives by the principle "I want to live a life of service" will act differently than a person who adheres to the principle "I'm only interested in what's good for me." And principles are revealed in our actions more than our words: though you might think you live by the principle "I'm always honest," for example, you may prove otherwise when someone asks, "Did you like my presentation?"

Principles provide us with a theoretical framework for being, but they are also very practical. They help us determine what to do in new or ambiguous situations. For example, if we embody the Partnership Principle of voice (see below) in our behavior, we do our best to talk and act in ways that show our conversation partners we believe their opinions matter.

Principles also help us describe both the person we are and the person we want to be. Though stating aloud that others matter doesn't magically turn us into people who listen with empathy, it does provide us with a starting point, a way to reflect on our practice, and, often, a way to diagnose where we need to do more work so that others see that we respect them, believe in them, and have their best interests at heart.

The Partnership Principles
Equality

The Universal Declaration of Human Rights begins with this statement: "Whereas recognition of the inherent dignity and of the equal and inalienable rights of all members of the human family is the foundation of freedom, justice and peace in the world...." That same principle drives the approach that I think coaches should take when partnering with teachers. When coaches work from the principle of equality, collaborating teachers feel seen, valued, and respected and believe they are afforded the status they deserve as professionals.

To embrace equality is to believe that no one person is more valuable than any other. As Nelson Mandela said, "The world's problems begin with the notion that some lives are more valuable than others" (Hatang & Venter, 2011). However, this doesn't mean that everyone should be treated the same. People are as unique as their fingerprints, with their own individual sets of strengths, needs, characteristics, and histories, so it would be unfair and ineffective to treat them interchangeably. Indeed, if we work from the belief that everyone is equally valuable, we should feel compelled to support policies and practices that differentiate for each person.

Equality and resistance. In their landmark book *Motivational Interviewing* (2013), about an approach to therapy that is grounded in the principle of equality, William Miller and Stephen Rollnick write that few people "appreciate… the extent to which change talk and resistance are substantially influenced by counseling style. Counsel in a directive, confrontational manner, and client resistance goes up. Counsel in a reflective, supportive manner, and resistance goes down while change talk increases" (p. 9). When we work from the principle of equality, we see the unique aspects of each person. We don't see others as stereotypes—a new teacher, a special education teacher, a resistant teacher; instead, we see Keysha, Suzanne, or Kurt. We affirm, we show respect, we listen, and, perhaps most important, we remain fully present in conversations because we believe the other person counts.

Saying we believe in equality is easy, but our words can give us away if we don't live up to them. In the many workshops I've led, the way people talk suggests that they are only able to pay lip service to equality as a principle. Questions like "What if the teacher doesn't take my advice?" "What if the teacher's opinion is wrong?" and "What if the teacher picks the wrong strategy to move toward the goal?" are really telegraphing that their suggestions are always superior to the teachers' and that the teachers should always implement them.

While our experience and expertise may enable us to see things that others don't, research suggests that our observations aren't as accurate as we think. Most of us of tend to overestimate the value of our insights, for example (Buckingham & Goodall, 2019). Further, telling people what to do creates dependency by communicating that we don't think they are capable of solving problems on their own.

Equality and moralistic judgment. We violate the principle of equality when we moralistically judge collaborating teachers, thinking or even claiming that they are not as good as we are. In his book *The Six Secrets of Change* (2008), Michael Fullan describes moralistic judgment, which he calls *judgmentalism,* as follows:

Judgmentalism is not just seeing something as unacceptable or ineffective. It is that, but it is particularly harmful when it is accompanied by pejorative stigma, if you will excuse the redundancy. The advice here, especially for a new leader, is don't roll your eyes on day one when you see practice that is less than effective by your standards. Instead, invest in capacity building while suspending short-term judgment. (p. 58)

Moralistic judgment contradicts equality by placing others below us. That creates a gap between us and them that kills intimacy and prevents learning. We don't run to get help from someone who will roll their eyes when we talk (and as I've heard Michael Fullan say in his presentations, there are many ways to "roll your eyes" without using your *actual* eyes).

Avoiding moralistic judgment does not mean avoiding reality. A clear picture of reality is essential for growth and learning. We can talk about reality and avoid judgment by communicating that we respect and believe in the teachers with whom we work. During a conversation based on equality, there is energy, openness, and a mutual sharing of ideas in part because the coach believes teachers should choose their paths for themselves.

Choice

When coaches embrace the principle of choice, teachers make most, if not all, of the decisions about changes to their classrooms. There is freedom in the conversation that isn't possible when coaches try to control what teachers do. When a conversation feels "off" or "out of sync," it is often because collaborating teachers don't feel they are free to say, do, or think what is on their minds.

What the research says about choice. Working from the principle of choice is not just a nice thing to do but a practical necessity. More than three decades of research has shown that telling professionals what to do without giving them a choice almost always results in failure. Researchers such as Teresa Amabile, Regina Conti, Heather Coon, Jeffrey Lazenby, and Michael Herron (1996); Edward Deci and Richard Ryan (2017); and Martin Seligman (2011) all consider autonomy to be essential for motivation. Deci and Ryan characterize the conclusions they've drawn from decades of research as *social determination theory*—namely, the idea that people feel motivated when they

(1) are competent at what they do, (2) have a large measure of control over their lives, and (3) are engaged in and experience positive relationships. The theory posits that the opposite is also true: when people are controlled and told what to do, are not in situations where they can increase their competence, and are not experiencing positive relationships, their motivation will be "crushed" (Ryan & Deci, 2000, p. 68).

A report from the Institute of Educational Sciences (Malkus & Sparks, 2012) summarizes research showing the importance of teacher autonomy:

> Research finds that teacher autonomy is positively associated with teachers' job satisfaction and teacher retention (Guarino, Santibañez, and Daley 2006; Ingersoll and May 2012). Teachers who perceive that they have less autonomy are more likely to leave their positions, either by moving from one school to another or leaving the profession altogether (Berry, Smylie, and Fuller 2008; Boyd, Lankford, Loeb, and Wyckoff 2008; Ingersoll 2006; Ingersoll and May 2012). (p. 2)

Yet despite the important role of choice, research suggests that autonomy is decreasing for almost all teachers (Malkus & Sparks, 2012).

Why choice is important. Choice is essential for at least three reasons. First, top-down models of change usually do not work. Telling professionals what they have to do might yield compliance, but not commitment (Deci & Flaste, 2013). Many educators have experienced top-down initiatives that were rolled out with a lot of fanfare but wound up having little impact on how teachers teach and how students learn.

Second, controlling other people is dehumanizing. As Donald Miller has written, "the opposite of love is ... control" (2015). Our ability to make choices largely defines our humanity. When we tell people they have no choice, we take away their ability to choose to commit—and, more important, to think for themselves. "Saying no is the fundamental way we have of differentiating ourselves," writes Peter Block. "If we cannot say no, then saying yes has no meaning" (1993, p. 29).

Finally, choice is essential for accountability. We might think that accountability refers to people doing what they are told, but I refer to this as *irresponsible accountability* because it leaves out the crucial factor of personal responsibility. A few years back, at our intensive coaching institute in

Kansas, one instructional coach painted a vivid picture of what irresponsible accountability can look like in our schools: "Our principal went to a teacher to talk about her students' low achievement scores," she said. "When the principal raised the topic of the scores, the teacher pointed out that she was implementing the program the district had told her to implement. 'I did everything I was told to do, and I did it with fidelity,' she said. 'If my students aren't doing well, I'm not the problem—it's your program.'"

Responsible accountability is different. When educators are responsibly accountable, their professional learning has an unmistakable impact on student learning, making them accountable to students, parents, fellow educators, and other stakeholders. Further, at the individual or school level, responsible accountability represents a genuine commitment, both individually and collectively, to professional learning and growth—a recognition that, to have learning students, we need to also have learning teachers, learning coaches, and learning administrators. In short, responsible accountability is essential for professional learning—and it isn't possible without choice.

What choice is not. Research suggests that choice is essential, but that's not the same as saying "anything goes." Choice does not mean that teachers can bully students, lose assignments, or be toxic members of a team. Choice also does not mean that teachers can choose to ignore district initiatives, skip over nonnegotiables, or stop learning. Choice need not lead to incoherence, either. Indeed, true coherence requires commitment, and commitment requires choice. There will be better implementation and deeper commitment to coherence when teachers have an authentic voice in making the decisions that matter most to them.

Instructional coaching done well produces measurable improvements that lead to better learning and better lives for students. It also ensures that teachers set their own goals, choose the strategies they'll use to meet those goals, monitor progress, and determine for themselves when their goals have been met. Further, coaches honor teacher autonomy by ensuring that teachers' voices are heard.

Voice

When coaches work from the principle of voice, they listen to teachers because they believe that their opinions matter. Teachers' thoughts, words, ideas, and emotions genuinely shape the conversations and actions that occur during coaching.

Voice is the natural outcome of a commitment to equality and choice. If coaches truly see their collaborating teachers as important, and if they are truly committed to teachers making the decisions about what happens in their classrooms, then naturally coaches need to hear what teachers think. As Quaglia and Corso (2014) have noted, teachers should be "the subject of their activities, not the object of someone else's" (p. 2).

Unfortunately, truly hearing someone else has become increasingly rare. The famous people we watch communicating on our various screens rarely listen carefully, and interruptions are the norm. Too often it's the loudest voice, not the wisest, that wins the argument. This is because people associate the loudest voice with confidence. And if we are struggling to hold things together ourselves, we can be drawn to confidence, even arrogance, because it makes us feel like those who exhibit it have a way out of whatever complex challenge we are facing. But arrogance often leads to simplistic thinking, and the complex work of inspiring students to learn and grow is rarely addressed with clichés and quick fixes.

Unfortunately, evidence suggests that most of us aren't really interested in hearing others' opinions. Despite social media's potential for democratizing discourse around important topics, in reality, it often seems more about pushing out a carefully crafted message than taking in what others are saying. It is about voice, but only *my* voice.

Marcus Buckingham and Curt Coffman (1999) surveyed more than a million employees and interviewed more than 80,000 managers to create a short list of factors that ensure an engaged, successful, happy, and productive staff. One of those factors was voice. Successful employees, they found, answer yes to the question "At work, do you feel like your opinions count?"

Gallup researcher Shane Lopez explored the idea of voice further. He surveyed doctors, nurses, truck drivers, restaurant employees, miners, teachers, and other workers to find out whether they felt their voice mattered at work. The day before Gallup released his research, Shane and I happened to meet at a little restaurant in Lawrence, where we both lived. When I asked him about his findings, he leaned across the table and said, "You won't believe who felt that their voice counted the least. Teachers." As Shane and Preety Sidhu write in their paper about their research on voice, "Despite having higher engagement than the national average, teachers are the least likely of all occupations to say 'at work my opinions seem to count'" (Lopez & Sidhu, 2013, para. 7).

And teachers are not alone in feeling like they don't have a voice in school. As Quaglia and Corso (2014) have noted, student voice is also "not yet a reality in most classrooms and schools." Quaglia and Corso partnered with Pearson Education to conduct a national survey of over 56,000 students in grades 6 through 12. The results showed that only 46 percent of students felt they had "a voice in decision making at their school" and only 52 percent believed "that teachers are willing to learn from students." A mere 45 percent of students considered themselves "valued members of their school community... even though 94 [percent believed they could] succeed and 67 [percent saw] themselves as leaders" (p. 2). Quaglia and Corso summed up their findings as follows:

> There may be thousands of students in our schools, maybe hundreds in any particular school, who, confident in their ability to succeed and ready to lead, feel shut out by adults they perceive as unprepared to listen to or value their ideas. (p. 2)

When I asked Russ Quaglia if there was a relationship between teacher voice and student voice, he was unequivocal: "Absolutely. When teachers don't have a voice, students don't have a voice, but when teachers *do* have a voice, students do, too—and when they do, they are five times more likely to feel engaged in school."

Honoring others' voices is essential, but that doesn't mean coaches can't share what they are thinking during a conversation. It just means they need to communicate in a manner that honors the thinking ability of their collaborating teacher. This ability to share ideas in a way that opens up conversation—to engage in a dialogue where people think together creatively—is an essential part of coaching.

Dialogue

Working from the principle of dialogue means the coach and teacher really hear each other and ideas flow so fluidly between them that both are energized by the thrill of learning, reflection, and creation. In this way, dialogue is life-giving.

When we commit to the principle of dialogue, we embrace a way of interacting that is grounded in respect for others. We enter into conversations intent to learn from our conversation partners. In doing so, we let go of the need to force our truth onto others and choose instead to critically explore our ideas with them. Dialogue involves genuine curiosity and an authentic commitment to learning, and it is only possible when we let go of the *need* to be right so that we can *do* what is right.

Peter Senge's *The Fifth Discipline* (1990) helped me see the potential of dialogue as a mutually humanizing form of communication in organizations. Through dialogue, Senge writes, "people continually expand their capacity to create the results they truly desire, where new and expansive patterns of thinking are nurtured, where collective aspiration is set free, and where people are continually learning how to learn together" (p. 3). Later, he adds that "all of us have had some taste of dialogue—in special conversations that begin to have a life of their own, taking us in directions we could never have imagined nor planned in advance" (p. 239).

The book that has most focused my thinking about dialogue is Paulo Freire's *Pedagogy of the Oppressed* (1970), in which Freire describes love, humility, faith, trust, hope, and critical thinking as necessary conditions for love.

Love. "Love," Freire writes, "is the foundation of dialogue... [because dialogue] cannot exist... in the absence of a profound love for the world and for [people]" (p. 77). This is a challenging statement, in part, because the word *love* has been so trivialized that it has lost much of its meaning. My definition is shaped particularly by Thomas Oord, who writes that "to love is to act intentionally, in sympathetic response to others... to promote well-being" (2005, p. 919). Simply put, when people "act intentionally... to promote well-being" of others, the opportunity for dialogue presents itself. Love is a prerequisite for dialogue.

Humility. "Dialogue," Freire writes, "cannot exist without humility" (p. 78). Since dialogue is a back-and-forth form of conversation, we need to enter it open to changing, perhaps even expecting to change, our opinions. People who are sure they are right and who aren't interested in learning from others won't experience genuine dialogue.

To be humble doesn't mean we choose to have low self-efficacy (or worse, that we *pretend* to have low self-efficacy). We should believe in our ideas and be open to learning and willing to be wrong. When we approach others with a desire to hear what they have to say rather than with a desire to put them in their place, then we are moving toward a more dialogical way of being.

Faith. "Faith in [people]," Freire writes, "is an *a priori* requirement for dialogue; the dialogical [person] believes in other [people] even before he meets them face to face" (p. 79). Simply put, if we are going to have dialogue with people, we need to believe in them. If we dismiss them as having nothing to teach us, then dialogue is pretty much impossible.

One way to understand what it means to believe in people is to consider what it looks like when we *don't*. If we see conversation as a one-way interaction with the goal to give advice, tell people what they've done right and wrong, and dictate what their next steps should be, we won't experience dialogue. A school where professional development is designed to tell teachers what to do is often one where teachers eventually stop thinking for themselves and say to the coach, "Just tell me what to do, and I'll do it." When we believe in others, we see them as people who want to do good and who can teach us something. We approach them from the perspective of learners, not judgers.

Trust. When we approach others with love, humility, and faith, trust is the natural outcome. As Freire writes, "it would be a contradiction in terms if dialogue—loving, humble, and full of faith—did not produce this climate of mutual trust" (p. 80). Trust is established by dialogue, but it will be diminished or destroyed without love, humility, and faith. "False love, false humility, and feeble faith in [people] cannot inspire trust" (p. 80).

Hope. "Dialogue," Freire writes, "cannot exist without hope" (p. 80). If people have given up believing that a situation can improve and blame others or simply complain, they are not engaging in dialogue. A constructive dialogue is about what we *can* do, not why we *can't* do things. "Hopelessness is a form of silence," writes Freire, "of denying the world and fleeing from it" (p. 80). Dialogue, by contrast, is a conversation about a better possible future, and consequently not only requires but also nurtures hope.

Critical thinking. Finally, dialogue involves critical thinking. Drawing on the work of Bohm (1996), Peter Senge (1990) writes that the purpose of dialogue "is to go beyond any one individual's understanding" (p. 241). Such learning involves critical thinking and conversations that push us to reflect deeply on our current reality, surfacing what Bohm calls "the incoherence in our own thought" (p. 81).

We can't succeed at this kind of thinking on our own. We learn about our incoherence by talking with other people, through the back and forth of ideas at the heart of dialogue. It is in dialogue, Senge writes, that "people become observers of their own thinking" (p. 242)—a process we refer to as *reflection*.

Reflection

Coaches who work from the principle of reflection empower teachers to think deeply about what has happened in the past, what is happening in the present, and what will happen in the future. As educational consultant Lou Mycroft has said, coaching is where teachers should "do their best thinking." As I first wrote in *Unmistakable Impact* (Knight, 2011), reflection can be described as having three dimensions: looking back, looking at, and looking ahead.

1. *Looking back* is reflection focused on considering how something went. Many coaching conversations involve this kind of conversation, looking back on a lesson or an event to consider what went well, what didn't go so well, and what the collaborating teacher might want to change before the next lesson.

2. *Looking at* is reflection that occurs in the moment. For example, a teacher might decide to spend more time on a classroom discussion than planned after realizing that the discussion is leading students to some new insights. Most teachers do this kind of thinking all day, adjusting lessons as they teach so that students learn more and experience greater well-being.

3. *Looking ahead* means considering how an idea, a strategy, or a tool might be used in the future. For example, a science teacher partnering with a coach might "look ahead" to plan how students will create concept maps that deepen their knowledge, to decide which students will

work best together in which groups, or to determine how to differentiate learning for individual students.

To ensure that teachers do a lot of thinking, coaches need to resist the
temptation to give advice. When coaches take a top-down approach, telling
teachers what to do, they create dependency and rob teachers of the chance
to think for themselves.

Praxis

When coaches work from the principle of praxis, learning is grounded in
and shaped by the realities of the collaborating teacher's classroom and life.
Teachers are usually fully engaged in the learning because it addresses something important to them—typically better student learning or well-being. As
such, praxis is learning in action.

The word *praxis* has been in use ever since Aristotle (1961) coined it
more than 2,000 years ago to identify one of what he considered to be the
three basic human activities: (1) *theoria* (thinking), (2) *poiesis* (doing), and
(3) *praxis* (acting). The term has been used in many ways since then, but
almost always to describe an experience that combines reflection and action.
As I use it, *praxis* describes any experience that combines reflection, learning, and action. It is the creative act of applying an idea to an important, real
situation. Praxis compels people to bring their true selves to whatever they
are doing because what they are doing is authentic. You can't fake it—either
the learning is real, or it isn't praxis.

This may all sound a little highfalutin, but praxis is by definition grounded
in reality. People's hands should be dirty, so to speak, from wrestling with
ideas. Thus, praxis, as I describe it, is usually driven by a real issue a person is
addressing. For example, a teacher might identify that many of her students
don't feel psychologically safe in her classroom and partner with a coach to
address this by establishing and reinforcing classroom norms for safety.

Authors like Paulo Freire (1970) and Hannah Arendt (1958) have
described praxis as an essential part of our humanity. In contrast, systems
that take away our ability to creatively interact with ideas and apply them to
our work and personal lives—that is, to what Arendt calls the "vita activa"—
are dehumanizing.

Teachers who are engaged in praxis are learning and thinking through how to apply some new knowledge to real-life classroom experiences. According to Freire (1970), praxis should lead us to analyze our lives and the world around us so we can change both ourselves and the world. That is why Freire considers praxis revolutionary. "[I]t is reflection and action upon the world in order to transform it," he writes. "To speak a true word is to transform the world" (p. 75).

Too often, we design professional development without considering the concept of praxis—we tell teachers what to do and how to do it, leaving little room for the creativity and knowledge teachers bring to school. To bring about the schools our children deserve, we need to ensure that teachers don't turn their brains off when they walk into our buildings. To that end, professional development that is designed with praxis in mind brings the creative thinking of teachers to life. Teachers don't unthinkingly implement what they've been told to implement; rather, they draw upon all they know to create something important—a great learning experience for their students.

Reciprocity

When coaching is grounded in the principle of reciprocity, coaches and teachers learn together. Coaches seek out and value the ideas teachers share, and teachers learn from coaches. The way coaches talk, listen, and act reveals that coaches are truly learning from teachers.

Some learning requires at least two people; it requires the second set of eyes or hands that a coach brings to our work and life. I see this during our workshops on coaching when I ask participants to coach each other on some issue. For the activity, which Michael Bungay Stanier developed and which he has generously allowed me to use, I post some of the questions from Michael's book *The Coaching Habit* (2016) and then have partners ask them of each other. The main rule of the activity is that those asking the questions can't speak after they have asked the questions. Each person takes turns asking questions and listening, moving back and forth through five questions.

What fascinates me about these micro-coaching sessions is that even though the coach does nothing more than ask a question and listen, participants almost always report that they find the conversations very valuable.

This has led me to wonder whether people would arrive at the same conclusions if they asked themselves the questions without a partner. But when I ask my workshop participants if people could just coach themselves, they always answer that they need another person to act as a sounding board, to listen, to nonverbally communicate concern, and to serve as an audience for their learning. The kind of learning that comes from coaching, it seems, is less likely to happen without a learning partner.

Coaches who work from the principle of reciprocity get as much as they give during coaching conversations. When they enter into these conversations curious and expecting to learn, they are usually rewarded. Everyone has something to teach us, and one of the joys of the partnership approach is that it makes it much more likely that we will learn from and with teachers. When the coach and teacher learn together, they share the joy of discovery, mutual exploration, and learning—and students reap the benefits.

To Sum Up

The Partnership Principles represent one possible set of principles to guide instructional coaching. Since one of the principles is choice, it would be staggeringly hypocritical of me to suggest that coaches must work from this specific set alone, but our research and experience do suggest that coaches will be more successful if they ground their work in the following seven beliefs:

- **Equality:** I don't believe any person or group is more valuable than any other, and I recognize and honor the dignity of every individual.
- **Choice:** I communicate in a way that acknowledges the professional discretion of others by positioning them as decision makers.
- **Voice:** I want to hear what others have to say, and I communicate that clearly.
- **Dialogue:** I believe conversations should consist of a back-and-forth exchange, with all parties hearing and responding to one another's opinions.
- **Reflection:** I engage in conversations that *look back, look at,* and *look ahead.*
- **Praxis:** I structure learning so that it is grounded in real life.
- **Reciprocity:** I enter each conversation open and expecting to learn.

Reflection Questions

Equality

1. What can you do to be fully present in conversations?
2. How easy is it for you to avoid moralistic judgment? What can you do to be less judgmental?
3. What are some subtle ways that you might be communicating that you don't see your collaborating teachers as equals? Do you think you engage in any of these behaviors? Do you want to change this?

Choice

1. To what extent do teachers make the decisions about what happens in their classrooms when you coach?
2. How do you go about explaining strategies while also honoring teacher choice?

Voice

1. Who does most of the talking when you are coaching? Do you need to change anything?
2. What do you do to ensure that you deeply understand the emotions and needs of your conversation partners?
3. What do you do to ensure that your collaborating teachers know that they have been heard?

Dialogue

1. Do you think dialogue is necessary for coaching? Why or why not?
2. Do you think it is important to demonstrate love, humility, and faith to collaborating teachers during coaching? If so, how do you demonstrate those qualities?
3. In your experience, what are the characteristics of a life-giving conversation?
4. In your organization, are teachers irresponsibly or responsibly accountable? What do you see in teachers' behavior that supports your answer?

Reflection
1. How easy is it for you to let your teachers make the decisions about what happens in their classroom?
2. When are you most reflective? How much time do you set aside to look back, look at, and look ahead?
3. What difference would it make if you spent more time reflecting on your personal and professional life?

Praxis
1. What can you do to ensure that the professional development you provide genuinely addresses teachers' real-life concerns?
2. What does it look like when teachers enthusiastically implement the ideas you discover and create together? What can you do to ensure that happens more often?
3. What can you do to ensure that professional development is guided by teachers' concerns?

Reciprocity
1. Do you believe you can learn from every single teacher with whom you partner?
2. Are your collaborating teachers energized by your coaching conversations? Are you?

Going Deeper

- I first read *Pedagogy of the Oppressed* (Freire, 1970) in a philosophy of education class when I was 19 years old. The book changed my view of the world then, and it continues to shape my thinking now. It isn't an easy read, but it is worth the effort because it might change your life, too.
- Peter Block's *Stewardship* (1993) started me thinking and talking about partnership as a model for human interaction. I now use the term *partnership* just about every time I talk with groups of people.
- Daniel Pink's *Drive* (2009) is a must-read if you want to understand why telling people what to do almost guarantees they won't do it. Pink's

book offers an accessible and useful overview of more than 30 years of research on human motivation.

- Ryan Holiday's *Ego Is the Enemy* (2016) is an inspiring treatise on why ego almost always stands at the heart of the messes we experience in life and work—a strong argument for the partnership approach to human interaction. Holiday explains why ego is so destructive and then explains what we can do to keep ours under wraps.

- Adam Grant's *Give and Take: Why Helping Others Drives Our Success* (2014) offers an evidence-based argument for reciprocity. Chances are it will encourage you to be more generous in all aspects of your life. At least, that's how it has affected me.

What's Next?

The Partnership Principles are deceptively easy to accept. Most people find it easy to acknowledge that everyone should have a voice and that we should all learn from each other. The challenge lies in understanding our relationships as involving an equal distribution of power. As Peter Block (1993) writes, "Partnership means to be connected to one another in a way that the power between us is roughly balanced" (p. 28).

When you consider adopting the Partnership Principles, ask yourself, "Am I really willing and able to give up control? Am I committed to letting my collaborating teachers make the decisions about what they do in their classrooms?" Answer these questions by deeply examining your thoughts, words, and actions. Video can be a huge help with this kind of learning because it allows us to watch our coaching conversations and see if we listened more than we talked, gave advice, or balanced telling with asking.

Partnership can seem like a paradox, but that doesn't make it any less true that the more we stop trying to influence others, the more influence we likely will have.

Learning Map for Chapter 2

Communication Skills

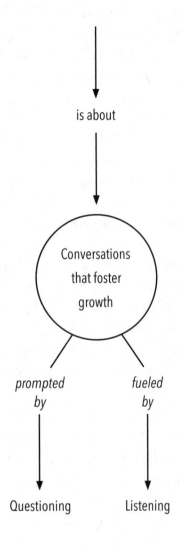

is about

Conversations
that foster
growth

*prompted
by*

*fueled
by*

Questioning

Listening

2 Communication Skills

Listening moves us closer, it helps us become more whole, more healthy, more holy.
Not listening creates fragmentation, and fragmentation is the root of all suffering.

—Margaret Wheatley, *Turning to One Another*

Like many other instructional coaches, Angela Adams never expected to leave the classroom. "I blissfully taught 6th and 8th grade science for 20 years and never gave a single thought to not teaching because I loved it so much," Angela told me. "When I say [quitting] never occurred to me, I mean it literally *never* occurred to me."

However, in her 20th year of teaching, Angela "started paying attention to how many teachers were leaving the classroom" and realized they were "dropping like flies." At first, she assumed teachers were quitting because of low pay, but when she talked with them, she discovered it was due to the day-to-day disappointments of the job. They had trouble controlling the kids, didn't feel like they were making a difference, or weren't teaching as much as they thought they'd be. Angela couldn't change people's salaries, but she believed she could help them with their classroom experiences. "As soon as I started talking to them, I thought, 'Well, I could actually help with that.'"

Angela applied for and was hired as a lead coach for the University of South Carolina Teacher Induction Program. Her job, she told us, was "to stick with new graduates for the first three years they are in classrooms, a time period research tells us is crucial when it comes to staying in education." But Angela quickly learned that her job involved a lot more than sharing effective instructional strategies:

> The first year of the program is what we would call emotional engagement; it's working with decisions such as "I'm calling off my engagement, I think I might be pregnant, I want to move out of my parents' house"—you know, that kind of stuff, which everyone goes through no matter what their occupation is.... And then generally by year two we are moving to the instructional coaching because we have normally gotten past the emotional stuff, then by year three our goal is to turn participants into teacher leaders. We

want them to stay teachers forever and be the types of teachers who would volunteer to be department heads or team leaders.

To help us understand what Angela does as a lead coach, she told us a story about her kindergarten teacher, Ms. Shepard. When Angela was 5 years old, her world revolved around Ms. Shepard. "I loved her so much," Angela told us, "and I was pretty sure I could make her love me as long as I finished everything faster than anyone else."

One day, after Angela rushed through an assignment and made a number of mistakes, Ms. Shepard asked her to redo the task. Instead of redoing the entire assignment, Angela cut and pasted the correct parts of her old assignment onto the new assignment. "Complete cheating," Angela said. "The paper probably looked like a wolverine had gotten hold of it. I took it to Ms. Shepard. She took one look at it and said, 'Angela, you are a problem solver.' Then she took the paper and put it in the 'done' stack."

Thirty-eight years later, Angela still thinks of herself as a problem solver. "It's like a tattoo on your heart," she says. Today, Angela tries to do for teachers what Ms. Shepard did for her when she was a little girl. "They are new and fresh, and what I have figured out is that we teach them the things that they will believe about themselves as teachers forever. I just want every teacher in every classroom to want to be there and to feel good about being a teacher."

And she's succeeding. Angela told me that over the first two years, 100 percent of teachers in her program—67 out of 67—continued in the classroom the following year. "A lot of the job is about relationships," Angela told me. "It's about late-night texts and teachers being upset, jilted, or whatever."

At the Instructional Coaching Group, we have discovered what Angela did: Relationships matter. Coaches need to communicate effectively, showing that they are trustworthy and that they care. As Angela says, "Coaching can be taught and it can be learned, but caring about teachers, remembering what it was like to be a teacher—that is very significant." Angela didn't worry about resistant teachers. She worried about understanding what her teachers needed and responding appropriately in the moment. And to understand the teachers with whom she partnered, Angela had to ask great questions and listen.

Questioning

My life partner, Jenny, likes to ask a question that always opens up conversations: "When you're not working, what do you like to do?" When she asks that question, it's like she's switched on the light in a dark room. People come alive and tell her about the joy they get from taking photographs, surfing, making their own beer, or whatever it is they love to do. That is how questioning should work during coaching, and why questioning is one of the most important coaching skills. I like to say that questions are to coaches what ice skating is to hockey players: if you want to play the game, you have to learn the skill.

Many have written about the importance of effective questions. Journalist Warren Berger writes that "the most creative and successful people tend to be expert questioners" (2014, p. 28). "All of our knowledge results from questions," writes Neil Postman, "which is another way of saying that question asking is our most important intellectual tool" (quoted in Sattes & Walsh, 2010, p. 28). Steve Barkley, who has been studying coaching for more than 30 years, says, "Questioning is the most critical of all coaching skills" (2011, p. xiii).

Great Questions

The best questions are like fertilizers for the garden of learning. They generate more ideas and deeper thoughts, and they are intellectually pleasurable to answer. A great question, Berger (2014) writes, "is hard and interesting enough that it is worth answering, and easy enough that one can actually answer it" (p. 8).

The best questions are short and clear and focus on the collaborating teacher rather than the questioner. Great questions don't show off the coach's brilliance, but they can empower others to have brilliant insights. They affirm, foster hope, and encourage others to see their strengths and successes. They often evoke a positive future rather than digging deeply into what isn't working. Great questions communicate respect, which means that they don't carry an implicit criticism like "Why aren't you giving students more feedback?" As coaching expert Julie Starr (2016) says, "Great questions avoid making somebody wrong" (p. 96).

When coaches ask effective questions, teachers become clearer about their options, and that clarity increases their energy. Great questions help teachers see more clearly what they can and cannot do and pin down the specific steps they will take to implement their plans.

Great questions are not one-size-fits-all. Coaches should choose the best question for a particular point in a conversation. Questions should be authentic; we sense when people are reading from a script, and most of us don't like to feel like we are being manipulated. This doesn't mean that coaches shouldn't find and remember favorite questions, but they should ask them authentically. Like jazz musicians who authentically play memorized riffs while improvising, coaches should pick and choose their questions and ask them at exactly the right time. A good question can move a conversation forward and create the opportunity for others to broaden their awareness, think deeply, plan, learn, and grow.

Open and Closed Questions

While there are many different kinds of coaching questions, people usually ask about one of three topics: how people *act* ("What is one step you can take to move closer to your goal?"), how they *feel* ("How did you feel when your students hit their goal?"), and what they *think* ("What surprised you this week?"). And within this framework, we usually ask two types of questions, either *open* ("How did you come to choose teaching as a career?") or *closed* ("When do you want to start using the strategy?"). Both kinds of questions are useful, but to be effective, they need to be used in the right situations at the right time.

That coaches should ask open questions might be the most common piece of advice I saw in the more than 50 books I reviewed for this chapter. Interestingly, there is no universal, precise definition of open and closed questions. My working definition of open questions is that they can elicit unlimited numbers of responses. For example, if I ask you, "What would you do if you were Secretary of Education?" you may have a long list of ideas to share. By contrast, closed questions elicit a limited number of usually short responses. For example, if I ask you, "Would you like to be the Secretary of Education?" you only have three possible answers: yes, no, or maybe.

Good open questions are both *evocative* and *generative:* evocative because they bring to light ideas, insights, emotions, and strategies, and generative because they can evoke an answer that leads to two ideas, then four, then eight, and so on. The best questions help us grow and see more than we otherwise would. When I ask an open question, I always feel a little excitement because I don't know how my partner will respond. It takes some courage to step off the beaten path of a planned conversation and potentially go where you've never gone before.

Whereas open questions invite teachers to think broadly and imagine possibilities, closed questions ask teachers to focus their thinking. Closed questions are good for beginning a conversation ("On a scale of 1 to 10, how would you rate your lesson?") or bringing one to an end ("Is there anything else we need to discuss?"). They can also be used to confirm that we understand what a teacher is saying ("Have I got that right?") or to confirm a teacher's commitment or confidence level ("On a scale of 1 to 10, how committed are you to the goal?").

As their names suggest, open questions open up conversations and closed questions narrow them down. This doesn't mean that open questions are better, just that the two types serve different purposes. It's up to coaches to decide when one makes more sense than the other.

Real Questions

The secret to asking great questions is to ask *real* questions. This might seem like a Zen koan, but the truth is we often make statements that only look like questions because they end with a question mark. "Don't you agree that your students need to have more input into what they learn?" isn't really a question; it is advice dressed up with interrogative punctuation. As Susan Scott has written, "When someone really asks, we really answer. And somehow both of us are validated" (2002, p. 94).

To ask real questions, we must avoid what are commonly referred to as *leading questions*—those that guide our conversation partners to a destination we have chosen for them (e.g., "Don't you think your students would learn more if they talked more?"). If we want to work in equal partnerships with collaborating teachers, we need to let go of the notion of leading them anywhere. When we ask questions that have solutions buried inside them, we take the responsibility for solving the problem away from teachers, thereby silencing them and probably diminishing their motivation. As journalist Kate Murphy (2019) writes, "Real questions don't have a hidden agenda of fixing, saving, advising, or correcting," but rather allow "people to tell their stories, express their realities, and find the resources within themselves to figure out how they feel about a problem and decide on next steps" (p. 147).

Real questions, then, are questions to which we don't know the answer; questions we ask because we are genuinely curious. Our curiosity shows teachers that they are important and we value what they have to say. Our curiosity also gives teachers the opportunity to be mutually curious and get wrapped up in the excitement of exploration. Michael Bungay Stanier (2020) advises coaches to be "relentless," staying "curious long enough to allow the other person to create the insight and space to reach the heart of the matter" (p. 85).

Deeper Questions

A large part of coaching involves thinking along with teachers and sometimes asking questions that let them think more deeply about a topic. A powerful question like Susan Scott's (2002) "Is it OK if nothing happens?" invites others to think deeper and notice important new insights.

To think with a collaborating teacher, the coach first needs to know what the teacher is saying and thinking. This is not as easy as it sounds. Listening and understanding are two different mental actions, and sometimes teachers move on to a new topic before coaches are sure what they mean. For this reason, coaches need to ask questions that clarify the collaborating teacher's thinking. Sometimes this means specifying what a teacher's words mean: "When you say *engagement,* what do you mean by that?" Other times, coaches need to listen for the message in the midst of a long, rambling statement. After a teacher has wound around a topic a fair bit, a coach may need to paraphrase what was said.

I often clarify what my conversation partner is saying for both our benefits. For example, I might ask, "Do you mind if I share what I'm hearing, and you can tell me if I've got it right?" When things are going well, my partner might say something like "That's exactly what I'm thinking, but you said it better than I was able to." Be sure to avoid using clarifying to redirect a conversation: if people think we are putting words in their mouth, they may see our listening as inauthentic and become uncomfortable. On the other hand, when people really feel heard, they relax, open up, and feel less pressure to push their message, making communication much more effective.

Some people refer to deeper questions as *probing questions*. However, like qualitative researcher Irving Seidman, I'm not fond of that terminology. "I always think of a sharp instrument pressing on soft flesh when I hear" the word *probe*, Seidman (2006) writes. "The word also conveys a sense of the powerful interviewer treating the participant as an object. I am more comfortable with the notion of exploring with the participant than with probing into what the participant says" (p. 86).

Rather than probing, I prefer to think of the coach as inviting the teacher to go deeper. Deeper questions don't probe; they invite collaborating teachers to unpack and explore their thoughts and statements. This can be accomplished by making simple suggestions or asking simple questions like "What else? Tell me more." Even a single response question ("Never?") can take a conversation deeper.

Asking and Responding

To ask good questions, coaches need to be intentional, choosing the right kind of question—open or closed—and the right topic (as noted earlier, usually thoughts, feelings, or actions). Though coaches must be curious, they need to ensure their curiosity doesn't lead them to ask questions that distract teachers from the topics they want to explore.

Coaches should ask short, simple questions that keep the focus on teachers' concerns. Many coaching experts suggest an 80-20 rule—coaches should talk no more than 20 percent of the time, freeing up the teacher to fill the other 80 percent.

Coaches need to make it easy for teachers to answer questions. To do this, they should acknowledge what teachers say using nonverbal gestures to communicate that they're listening. Often, these gestures are simply the natural result of a genuine desire to hear what their conversation partner has to say. Coaches should communicate that they are on the teacher's side by using words such as *we, us,* and *together*.

In their research on therapeutic relationships, William Miller and Stephen Rollnick (2013) distinguish between *consonant conversations,* where "there is a sense of moving together smoothly, like two dancers gliding across a ballroom floor," and *dissonant conversations,* where "counselor and client seem to be struggling against each other, grappling for control, like two adversaries in a wrestling match" (p. 43). "When a relationship is going dissonant," they say, "it is important to understand why":

> To use the term "resistance"... seems to suggest that things are not going smoothly because of something that one person [the client] is doing. We advocate a more relational view, in which client resistance behavior is, at most, a signal of dissonance in the relationship. In a way, it is oxymoronic to say that one person is not cooperating. It requires at least two people to not cooperate, to yield dissonance. (p. 45)

Blaming the other person turns our focus away from the one factor we are able to control with respect to resistance: ourselves. Rather than asking why people resist, a better question might be "What am I doing that is creating resistance?" or "How does the design of our professional development produce resistance?" In fact, rather than fighting resistance, a better strategy is to seek consonant conversations or what we might call alignment, conversations that are in sync.

Coaches can use the Partnership Principles to get in sync with others. When teachers feel they are equally important in a conversation—when they are heard, have a lot of autonomy, work on real-life issues, and partner with a coach who wants to learn from them—there is a good chance the conversation is in alignment. When coaching is working well, collaborating teachers freely say what they think, and the conversation productively moves in the direction they want it to move in.

Research shows that when a coach and teacher are in alignment, their brain waves are *literally* in sync. Summarizing the research of several neuroscientists, Kate Murphy (2019) explains: "Our brains not only sync up the moment someone tells us something, the resulting understanding and connection influences how we process subsequent information.... The more you listen to someone, such as a close friend or a family member, and the more that person listens to you, the more likely you two will be of like minds" (pp. 25–26). This is one reason why listening is such an important part of coaching.

Favorite Questions

In the second edition of *An Introduction to Coaching Skills* (2017), Christian van Nieuwerburgh suggests we gather our favorite questions. "As a coach, you find your own questions which are consistently helpful at different points in the conversation," he writes. "Very often, however, the most helpful question will emerge from a coachee's response if a coach is listening genuinely" (p. 50).

I've included many of my favorite questions throughout this book and especially in Chapter 4. In addition, you can download a more extensive list of my favorite questions at www.instructionalcoaching.com/bookstore/the-definitive-guide-to-instructional-coaching.

Listening
Listening as Improv

Kate Murphy (2019) proposes improvisational comedy, or improv, as a good analogy for listening. To deepen her understanding of this connection, she interviewed Matt Hovde, the artistic director at the famous Second City comedy club in Chicago. Hovde told Murphy that listening is "a fundamental skill" for improv actors, who "train ourselves to be very sensitive to what's happening on stage: to listen to what our scene partners are saying and what they mean, because if we miss those details, scenes will make less sense and will seem less magical or funny to an audience" (in Murphy, 2019, p. 106). Because improv performers don't know what they are going to do until someone else on stage says or does something, they need to constantly watch and listen so they can respond appropriately.

This makes them a lot like coaches. Just like improv actors, coaches must listen, draw from their experience, think quickly, and do the best they can in any given moment. However, coaches are not trying to entertain an audience; they are trying to set up the conditions for people to think and grow. To "think with" teachers, coaches need to know what collaborating teachers are thinking, and they won't know unless they listen to them.

Internal and External Dimensions of Listening

I find I am better able to improve my listening skills when I reflect on the *internal* and *external* dimensions of listening. Internal dimensions are the ways we control our thinking to better hear conversation partners; external dimensions are the words and actions we say and do that our partners observe during a conversation.

Internal

The internal dimensions of listening involve the internal monologues we engage in when we are listening and the thoughts that are too deep within us to be expressed as words. We need to become aware of those deeper thoughts, often referred to as *tacit knowledge,* or those unconscious ways of thinking can make it hard to hear others. To listen effectively, we need to mentally prepare ourselves to hear our conversation partners.

Focus. How we control what happens in our heads has a big impact on how well we listen—that is, on whether we are really focused on the other speaker. We all know we need to give our full attention to others, but most of us need to work at keeping our attention centered on what our conversation partners are communicating at any given time.

One reason we struggle to listen is that our brains move at a much faster speed than our conversation partner's speech. Kate Murphy (2019) refers to this disparity as the "speech-thought differential": "The average person talks at about 120–150 words per minute, which takes up a tiny fraction of our mental bandwidth powered by some eighty-six billion brain cells," she writes, so "when someone else talks, we take mental side trips" (pp. 70–71).

Technology can make us take mental side trips, too, by diverting our attention from conversation. Our smartphones and other devices are, in fact, designed to distract us (Eyal & Hoover, 2014). The little *bing* we hear when we get a text sends a dopamine hit to the happy place in our brain, and the more we use our phones, the more we crave that hit. Unfortunately, the quick moment of pleasure we get from reading our texts can damage our relationships if we're not careful. As Sherry Turkle says in *Reclaiming Conversation*

(2015), "Every time you check your phone in company, what you gain is a hit of stimulation, a neurochemical shot, and what you lose is what a friend, teacher, parent, lover, or co-worker just said, meant, felt" (p. 40).

While turning off our devices might be the first step toward focus, the second step is turning toward our conversation partner. We need to shut down the distracting voice in our head that fills us with irrelevant questions, assumptions, predictions, and other distracting thoughts. To really listen, we need to ask a question, let our conversation partners talk, and keep our mental focus on what they say. To paraphrase Stephen Covey (1989), we need to stop listening to reply, and start listening to understand.

Notice. Coaching expert Christian van Nieuwerburgh (2017) describes noticing as an important communication skill. In part, noticing means focusing on our partners: We need to pay attention to their nonverbal communication, noticing when they light up as they talk about a topic, when they hesitate or look somewhat confused, when their body language is inconsistent with the words they are saying. We should also be watching for strengths that come out in what a person says, so that we can highlight those strengths when appropriate. Indeed, nonverbal communication can reveal something about how aligned our learning partner is with us.

We should also pay attention to what is going on inside ourselves during a conversation, which we can do by reflecting on a few questions in the moment: "Do I feel like I am in alignment with the teacher?" "Do I feel comfortable or uncomfortable?" "Am I struggling to communicate, or am I finding it easy to find the right words?" "Do I feel like the teacher trusts me and feels safe with me, and are we both focused on the same goal?" Of course, we also shouldn't go so deep into our reflections that we stop noticing our conversation partner.

Don't make assumptions. Another way to keep our minds focused on what people really say is to not make assumptions. It is easy to understand why we tend to assume things: as human beings, when confronted with information, we automatically try to make sense of it. Unfortunately, we too often forget that assumptions are just guesses and start to take them as truths—and that can cause a lot of trouble. As Miguel Ruiz (1997) has written, "We make assumptions about what others are doing or thinking—we take it personally—then we blame them and react by sending emotional poison with our words.... We make an assumption, we misunderstand, we take it personally, and we end up creating a whole big drama for nothing" (p. 63).

Let's consider a coach who is working with a teacher who isn't implementing the strategies she had told the coach she would implement. Whenever the coach asks about the strategies, the teacher redirects the conversation and, as a result, the coach is worried she has wasted her time working with the teacher. In such a situation, it is easy for the coach to make all kinds of assumptions—that the teacher is a resistant person, or doesn't like her, or is lazy. Any of these assumptions would significantly interfere with the coach's ability to listen when she talks with the teacher.

A much better approach is to become aware of the assumptions you tend to make and stop making them. Instead, ask questions to find out what the teacher really thinks. If you talk with the teacher about a strategy and ask questions, you may find that she doesn't understand the strategy and is afraid of messing up in front of her students, or that she's facing personal issues that make it hard for her to implement anything new right now.

"Have the courage to ask questions until you are clear as you can be," writes Ruiz (1997), "and even then do not assume you know all there is to know about a given situation" (p. 72). To listen effectively, we need to unclutter our minds so that our assumptions don't interfere with our ability to understand the words, intentions, and actions of collaborating teachers.

Surface mental models. Our mental models can also keep us from hearing what others have to say. Peter Senge (1990) defines *mental models* as "our deeply held internal images of how the world works" (p. 174). Others use terms such as *paradigms, mindsets,* or *internal stories.* Whatever you call them, it is important to recognize mental models because they shape what we say and do. To control our mental models, we first need to interrogate ourselves to surface them. According to Senge, we need to "[slow] down our own thinking processes so that we can become more aware of how we form our mental models and how they influence our actions" (p. 191).

When we become aware of our mental models, we can listen with a clear mind, unencumbered by our assumptions. Consider, for example, the different ways coaches think, act, and talk if they have a fixed mindset versus a growth mindset. As Carol Dweck (2007) has famously explained, people with a fixed mindset believe their "qualities are carved in stone" (p. 6), whereas those with a growth mindset believe that "basic qualities are things you can cultivate through your efforts" (p. 7). Annie Brock and Heather Hundley (2016) further propose that coaches with growth mindsets will likely foster more growth than those with fixed mindsets.

Let go of control. One particularly distracting way of thinking is driven by our desire to get others to agree with us and do what we think is best. If we really want to hear others, we need to let go of the need to control conversations and let collaborating teachers speak and act as they choose.

Conversations, especially coaching conversations, can be ambiguous and messy. If we embrace the partnership approach, we won't know (and shouldn't *think* we know) what the teacher will say after we ask a question. Not knowing what will happen during coaching can feel stressful, and sometimes we may become overwhelmed by the temptation to take the conversation to a destination we choose. But if we do that, we aren't truly listening.

Demonstrate empathy. To demonstrate empathy, we need to understand the emotions and perspectives of others. We don't usually feel our partners' emotions as deeply as they feel them, but we can still feel something of what they feel and communicate to them that we understand. At the very least, we shouldn't ignore—or, worse, negate—our partners' emotions. Along with feelings, we need to understand our partners' perspective, which means we need to understand their needs. If we can both understand our partners' emotions and needs and communicate to them that we understand, our listening will be much more effective.

External

The external dimensions of listening are those that our coaching partners see and hear. It is not enough just to hear what people are saying; we also need to *show* that we are listening. Our actions, sometimes even more than our words, need to communicate that we hear what our conversation partners say. People who are sharing important information will be much more open if this is the case.

Be aware of nonverbal communication. One way to communicate that we are listening is to ensure that our body language shows we are focused on our conversation partner. We should make a respectful amount of eye contact (recognizing that eye contact is perceived differently within different cultures). We should turn our body toward our partner and take an open stance rather than sit with our arms crossed. Good listeners refrain from distracting gestures like clicking a pen, looking out the window, or checking a watch during the conversation. (If you've got a smartwatch, it can be especially challenging to not look at it when it vibrates or beeps.)

Be careful about taking notes. On the one hand, writing down what people say is a way of validating their ideas. On the other hand, if we focus too much on our notes, we may miss what people say or give the impression that we're not listening. My advice is to be judicious about when you take notes and to ask for permission. For example, when my conversation partner and I are exploring possible teaching strategies she might implement, I usually ask, "Do you mind if I make a list of the strategies we discuss?"

If you take notes on a tablet using a stylus and notetaking software, you can email the notes to your collaborating teacher as soon as the coaching conversation ends. In general, I advise against using any device with a keyboard to take notes, as it can make eye contact harder and serve as a physical barrier between coach and teacher.

Refrain from interrupting (unless absolutely necessary). Unfortunately, it has become more and more acceptable to interrupt in our society. On sports and political programs, for example, interruptions are the norm. Too often, the loudest and pushiest voice wins. But the ubiquity of interrupting doesn't make it an effective communication strategy. Indeed, I believe it is very destructive: when we interrupt, we are saying we don't think what the other person says is important—or, perhaps worse still, that we're more important than they are. Interrupting is clearly not consistent with the Partnership Principles.

Even if we think we're helping the other person, it's usually a good idea not to interrupt. As Christian van Nieuwerburgh (2017) explains, we shouldn't complete people's sentences or fill in the words they are trying to remember. Instead, van Nieuwerburgh writes, the goal of a coaching conversation should be to create a safe space for people to think. When we stop interrupting, we can, to quote Susan Scott (2002), "let the silence do the heavy lifting"—and let learning begin.

Despite these caveats, there *are* times when interrupting is necessary. If teachers spend a lot of time talking about a topic, for example, they may need to be reminded that there are only 10 minutes left until the bell and a goal hasn't been set yet. Other times, you may need to interrupt to clarify terminology or paraphrase just to make sure you understand what the other person is saying. In these moments, I suggest you do what Michael Bungay Stanier (2020) proposes: just tell them that you're interrupting. Say, "I'm just going to stop you for a moment" or "I'm going to hold you there." If you're in the room with the conversation partner or on video chat, you can hold your hand up to signal the interruption as well. Once the other person has stopped, say what you see: "I can hear there's a lot going on. In the interest of time, I'm going to force the issue here" (p. 105).

Although learning to interrupt effectively is important, refraining from interrupting except when absolutely necessary is more important. I have talked with many coaches who have identified not interrupting as an area for improvement after watching themselves on video. So far, no one has said, "You know what I need to do? I need to interrupt more."

Our goal as listeners is to ensure that our words and bodies communicate to our conversation partners that they have our attention. We must do everything we can to help people feel they are heard. Nonverbal communication and effective paraphrasing is never enough. What matters most is that we authentically want to hear what people have to say because we truly want them to flourish. Turning our attention to others is a powerful way to communicate that we have their best interests at heart. If our listening is guided by a genuine, respectful curiosity and benevolence, most of the skills and techniques of listening will naturally occur as we turn toward our conversation partners.

To Sum Up

To be effective coaches, we need to build relationships and trust—and to do that, we need to ask great questions and listen effectively. Great questions keep the focus of a conversation on the teacher; as Warren Berger (2014) writes, a great question "is hard and interesting enough that it is worth answering, and easy enough that one can actually answer it" (p. 8). Great questions authentically arise out of a coach's curiosity and interest in another person's well-being, in contrast to leading questions, which people use to lead others to destinations they have chosen for them. Great questions are short and appropriate to the moment—open questions to broaden conversations and closed ones to focus them. A great question should open up a conversation the way a light bulb opens up a dark room.

Listening can be understood as having internal and external dimensions. The internal dimensions of listening involve our internal monologues during conversations. Some important internal dimensions of listening include our ability to maintain our focus, notice our conversation partners and ourselves, avoid making assumptions, surface our mental models, and let go of the need to control our conversation partners. External dimensions of listening, by contrast, are what our conversation partners see and hear us say and do. These include our nonverbal communication, looking like we are listening, and not interrupting unless absolutely necessary.

Reflection Questions

1. How do you respond when teachers appear to be resisting change? Do you need to change anything about how to interact when you encounter resistance?
2. Is there anything you can do to increase teachers' hope?
3. What is your experience with change?
4. What do you think are the qualities of effective questions?
5. What do you do to create a safe place for your collaborating teachers to think?
6. Which questions have been most effective for you?
7. On a scale of 1 to 10, how effectively do you listen to your conversation partners?
8. What are one or two things you could do today to improve as a listener?
9. Do you do more telling than asking?
10. When you explain strategies, what can you do to move away from giving advice and toward a mutual exploration of ideas?

Going Deeper

- The books that most influenced what I have written here are Christian van Nieuwerburgh's *An Introduction to Coaching Skills* (2017) and William Miller and Stephen Rollnick's *Motivational Interviewing* (2013).

- Many of the ideas in this chapter are from my own book *Better Conversations* (2015).
- Beth Dankert Sattes and Jackie Acree Walsh's *Leading Through Quality Questioning* (2010) offers a great overview of the literature on questioning, along with many practical suggestions that any coach can use.
- Michael Bungay Stanier's *The Coaching Habit* (2016) has become an incredibly popular coaching book (maybe the most popular of all time), in large part because it describes seven effective coaching questions that any coach can use.
- Tony Stoltzfus's *Coaching Questions: A Coach's Guide to Powerful Asking Skills* (2008) is packed with dozens of great questions that could become part of any coach's question bank.
- Frank Sesno's *Ask More: The Power of Questions to Open Doors, Uncover Solutions, and Spark Change* (2017) provides another perspective on listening by offering a journalist's insight into questioning.
- My current favorite book on listening is Kate Murphy's *You're Not Listening* (2019), which offers an interesting and helpful overview of recent thinking about listening.
- Elena Aguilar's body of work is essential reading for any coach, and I could mention her work at the end of any of these chapters. Personally, however, I found her insights about questioning in *The Art of Coaching* to be especially helpful as I thought deeply about what good questions look like and how they can be asked respectfully and artfully during coaching and all other conversations.
- My all-time favorite book about listening and other communication topics is Margaret Wheatley's *Turning to One Another* (2002). Wheatley reminds us that "we can change the world if we start listening to one another again" (p. 3).

What's Next?

The easiest way for you to improve your coaching skills is to record a video of yourself in conversation. Watching a video of any conversation with anyone—your partner, child, colleagues, friends—can be helpful and sometimes even revelatory, but video of yourself coaching can be especially powerful. If your collaborating teachers agree to be recorded, I suggest watching at least one coaching conversation a week to assess how effectively you communicate.

Video can also be a big part of professional learning when coaches get together in PLCs or other groupings. Coaches can practice real-life facilitative coaching by using a coaching model such as the GROWTH model described in John Campbell and Christian van Nieuwerburgh's *The Leader's Guide to Coaching in Schools* (2018), the seven questions in Michael Bungay Stanier's *The Coaching Habit* (2016), or Sir John Whitmore's GROW model in *Coaching for Performance: The Principles and Practice of Coaching and Leadership* (2009).

Learning Map for Chapter 3

Coaches as Leaders

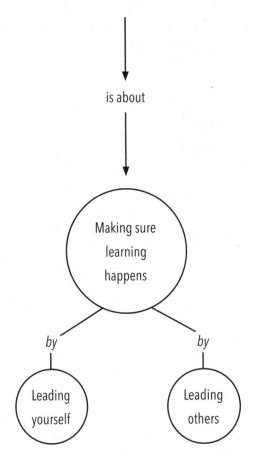

is about

Making sure learning happens

by

by

Leading yourself

Leading others

- Knowing your purpose
- Managing time
- Building habits
- Practicing self-care

- Balancing ambition with humility
- Being a Multiplier
- Creating alignment
- Making good decisions

3 Coaches as Leaders

[Your purpose] has to be something that doesn't allow you to sleep at night unless you're dreaming about it; something that wakes you up in the morning and gets you excited about it; or something that makes you so angry, you know you have to do something about it… because jumping from the "what" to the "do" is meaningless if you don't know why. Because when it gets hard, when it gets tough, when your friends walk away from you, when your supporters forget you, when you don't win your first race—if you don't know why, you can't try again.

—Stacey Abrams

Author and consultant Ann Hoffman, a longtime friend and colleague, has led workshops and provided coaching for thousands of educators around the world. Before writing books and consulting with educators, Ann was a special education teacher, and before that, she earned a graduate degree at the University of Iowa and an undergraduate degree at the University of Michigan in special and elementary education.

Going into special education was an easy choice for Ann. She grew up in a household where fighting for every person's human rights was a family value. Her sister was a volunteer who worked in the fields and eventually became an attorney for the United Farm Workers of America. Her mother was a member of the League of Women Voters and spoke out and protested for human rights so frequently that she and Ann's father were teased about her activism. Her father was "a kind, gentle soul" who was proud of Ann's mom's determination to do the right thing. "I was raised in a family where you give back to the community in which you live through behaviors and actions," Ann said.

Ann chose special education before the Individuals with Disabilities Education Act (IDEA) legislation was passed in 1975, at a time when many people with disabilities were institutionalized. "One of my best friends had a sister with Down syndrome, and I saw how the family refused to put her in an institution," she told me. "She was a part of the family, just like everybody else. It inspired me, seeing how they interacted with her. I remember reading about the institutions for people with disabilities, and it just broke my heart. So special ed has always just been what I wanted to do."

When Ann arrived at the University of Michigan as an undergraduate, she wanted to get her degree as quickly as possible so she could start teaching and making a difference. As soon as she got to campus, she met with her academic advisor and proceeded to plan out each course so that she knew exactly what she had to do to graduate. But on the day she went to register, Ann was surprised to see an unexpected course added to her schedule: Multicultural Education. She made it very clear to the registrar that she had a plan all worked out and that she was not excited that one more course had been added to her plan.

Just then, Ann heard a voice coming from an adjoining office: "Young lady, please come in here for a moment." Ann promptly went into the room, where she met Dr. Gwendolyn Calvert Baker, the director of affirmative action at the university. "I'm putting you in my class," she told Ann without further ado.

Dr. Baker was a pioneer at the University of Michigan. In her autobiography, she describes herself as a "a spirited black woman in a white world" (2014, p. 5). Dr. Baker never told Ann what to do or think, but she set up the conditions for Ann to learn for herself. She handpicked an inner-city school in Detroit for Ann to do her practicum, and here Ann saw firsthand the impact of structural racism. Students encountered roadblocks in the school that she had never seen before. They were learning from poor-quality basal readers printed on black-and-white newsprint, not the glossy full-color versions Ann had seen in suburban schools (she was shocked to hear them commonly referred to as "ghetto versions"). Many children didn't own coats, even though they came to school in the middle of frigid Detroit winters. At school, they sat in cold classrooms, often with boarded-up windows, as it was too costly to replace broken glass. In some classes, Ann watched students who had low spelling grades lined up in front of their classrooms and given the strap. "Students would start to cry as soon as they saw the grade on their test," Ann told me.

Heartbroken by what she had seen, Ann went to Dr. Baker's office in tears and asked naively, "Do you know what's happening in those schools?" Unperturbed, Dr. Baker answered, "Of course, I do; that's why you're there."

Eventually, Ann chose to do her student teaching in that same school, where she said she learned "as much or more" from her students as they did from her. "Through it all, Dr. Baker allowed me to see things through my eyes," she said. "She always treated me as an equal. Never less than. She never lectured me. She always let me speak and listened to me with compassion." Dr. Baker also invited Ann to join her family celebrations and brought her to conferences and lectures. Decades later, Ann still vividly remembers where she sat and what she heard about racism during those sessions. "Dr. Baker is the reason I wrote my first published paper on the topic of multiculturalism," she told me.

Ann was a different person when she left the University of Michigan. She had chosen Michigan because of the famous education professors who were teaching there at the time, but it was Dr. Baker who had the greatest impact on her life. "She changed me," Ann said. "My passion about fighting inequalities comes from her." Ann has subsequently passed on what she learned from Dr. Baker to the thousands of educators she coaches around the world. And those educators, in turn, are communicating to their students the fundamental beliefs that Ann shares—that every person matters and has dignity. Imagine the impact those tens of thousands of students will have with that knowledge and those values.

Dr. Gwendolyn Calvert Baker was only one person. But as her life shows, one person truly can make the world better. This is what leaders do. In critical moments and in simple but powerful ways, they change people's lives, and those changes affect others, and so on. As President Kennedy is reported to have said, "One person can make a difference, and every person should try."

Few people in the world are better positioned to make such a difference than coaches. Each time a coach partners with a teacher to bring about positive change, every student that teacher ever teaches benefits. In this way, in the course of just one year, one coach has a positive impact on thousands of children. A coach's impact should be measured by lifetimes, not one year's test scores!

The full extent of a coach's impact, of course, varies significantly from one coach to another, and this book is meant to discuss the many factors that either enhance or inhibit coaching success. However, when I sit in a room with a group of coaches who work in systems that support them and I learn that some are flourishing while others are struggling, the reason for that difference is often the same thing: leadership.

What *is* leadership? For many, leadership is about providing direction, clearly stating a vision or goal, and then motivating others to want to pursue that goal. Such a definition divides people into leaders and followers, suggesting that leadership is something people do to others by defining the direction they must take and motivating them to want to follow.

This definition is appropriate for some leaders, but for instructional coaches, a different model of leadership is more appropriate. Leadership based on the Partnership Principles involves helping others identify for themselves what they need to do rather than getting them to do what the leader has decided they should do. As such, leadership based on the Partnership Principles is an act of service, not control.

The leadership that coaches need to demonstrate involves two elements: leading yourself and leading others. We need to lead ourselves because, as Brené Brown (2018) writes, "who we are is how we lead" (p. 11). And we need to lead others so that, as educational consultant Kristin Anderson says, we can "help people unleash their brilliance."

Leading Yourself
Knowing Your Purpose

Simon Sinek's (2009) TEDxPugetSound presentation isn't that impressive if you only look at the external aspects of it. He is presenting at a small TEDx event, not the world-famous main conference. He is on a tiny stage, with a small audience, using a large handheld microphone instead of the more professional hands-free microphone that TED has made iconic. The lighting in the room is poor, and his only visual is a somewhat sloppy diagram he creates on chart paper. Truly, the overall look of the presentation doesn't blow you away.

Nevertheless, Sinek's TED Talk is one of the most popular ever. When I checked the TED website in early August 2020, it had been watched 51,002,062 times. That's twice the population of Australia! What makes it so popular? I believe it's the fact that it touches on a universal desire for a life that, as Sinek says, "starts with why."

Although Sinek's talk is about how leaders inspire action in organizations, his central idea—"start with why"—is, in the view of many, fundamental to living a fulfilling life. For example, Richard Leider asked thousands of people over the age of 65 to name one thing they wished they could do over in their lives. He ended up hearing so much about purpose that he wrote a book about it, *The Power of Purpose* (1997). And in one of the most powerful books of the 20th century, *Man's Search for Meaning* (1959), Viktor Frankl concluded that only purpose could get people through the ghastly, dehumanizing experiences of German concentration camps during World War II. Echoing Nietzsche, Frankl wrote that people "who know the why for [their] existence ... will be able to bear almost any 'how'" (p. 88).

One simple and powerful way to identify purpose comes from the island of Okinawa, Japan, home to the greatest number of centenarians in the world. Studying the residents on the island, Héctor García and Francesc Miralles found that the secret of a long and worthwhile life in Okinawa is wrapped up in one word: *ikigai*. "Our *ikigai*," the authors write in *Ikigai* (2016), "is hidden deep inside each of us.... According to those born on Okinawa, our *ikigai* can be simply understood as 'the reason we get up in the morning'" (p. 9). Figure 3.1, based on a diagram by Marc Winn, illustrates the four components of *ikigai:*

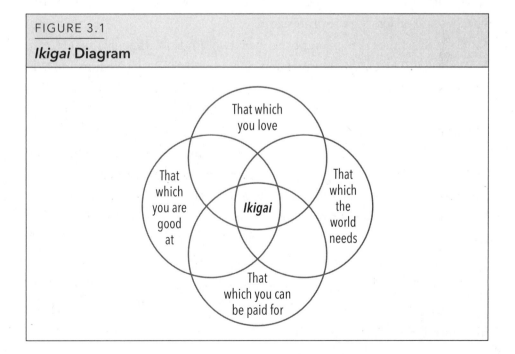

FIGURE 3.1

Ikigai Diagram

Understanding and embracing a purpose that is bigger than ourselves, like working to improve the quality of children's lives, moves us beyond our egos as we avoid the trap of worrying too much about our own interests. Trying to live a life motivated by ego is always a soul-crushing experience. By contrast, living a life of purpose helps us be more effective coaches and, more important, better people.

Managing Time

Coaches who understand their purpose increase the likelihood that they will have a positive impact on educators and students. However, they need to have the time to coach. It is hard to do the right thing when you don't have any time to do it.

Over the past few years, my colleagues and I at ICG have surveyed hundreds of coaches to learn about their experiences working in school, and the most frequent comment we have heard is that they simply don't have enough time to coach. Many coaches feel like they are trying to do the impossible, and faced with such a challenge, they try to multitask, cut corners, try harder, and work longer. Unfortunately, a lot of them end up feeling that they don't have time to do anything well. In fact, lack of time is likely one of the main reasons coaches end up leaving the profession.

Effective time management involves two kinds of dimensions: *external* and *internal*. The external dimension refers to all the tasks we must do that are outside our control. In Chapter 7, I explain in detail why administrators must partner with coaches to ensure that external demands on their time don't sabotage coaching efforts.

The internal dimension of time management refers to factors that coaches *can* control—the strategies they can use to set intentions, make plans, organize their calendars, reflect, and learn. There are at least five levels to this dimension: (1) *big picture,* (2) *middle view,* (3) *weekly,* (4) *daily,* and (5) *review.*

Big picture. Most time management experts suggest you start organizing your time by imagining a big picture of everything you want and need to do. If you have considered the four elements of *ikigai* depicted in Figure 3.1, you have already done a lot of this work.

In her book *Design the Life You Love* (2015), Ayse Birsel suggests designing a life map that depicts the most important parts of our lives to get an idea of "the big picture." Birsel suggests we start our map by listing the "ingredients" of our lives, then expanding on each ingredient by adding key words on a map, much like the learning maps that begin each chapter of this book. Maps and lists help us see the broad sweep of our lives before we write down what we have to do in the years, months, weeks, and days ahead.

Middle view. Once you understand your big picture, you can start to make more specific action plans for the coming year, quarter, and month. One way to do this is to create an annual list of benchmarks for the ingredients of your life. Of course, you may not want—or have the time—to do this kind of planning, so you may want to skip to weekly or daily planning. Each person has to create a system that works best for them.

One powerful strategy is to make appointments with yourself on your planner pages that show when you will actually do the actions you have identified. Nir Eyal (Eyal & Li, 2019) refers to this as "timeboxing." If you want to learn about a new strategy, create a video, write a paper for a graduate course, or even plan your year, you need to make time for that as an appointment on your calendar. If there's a scheduling conflict, then you need to reflect on your priorities and identify what you have to give up to be sure that you are doing what's most important or necessary. An appointment with yourself is just as important as any other appointment on your calendar. Once you make one, you have to show up and do what you have committed to do.

Weekly. You can use strategies like reviewing your *ikigai*, mapping, making lists, and timeboxing for weekly planning. I often make lists that include the people, roles, and projects I need to deal with. Many coaches list all the teachers they are partnering with and then write down the tasks they have to complete with each. In my experience, timeboxing is the most important part of the weekly plan because if you fail to schedule time for the most important tasks, the open slots will be picked off by less important tasks before you know it.

Daily. Almost every time management expert suggests identifying the two to four most important tasks (MITs) you need to accomplish every day, and then making sure that you do them no matter what else happens each day. Coaches may also want to identify MVPs—the most valuable people with whom they need to partner.

Review. Before you plan your day, you may want to look back on the previous day to see if you need to change anything. So-called "after-action review" (AAR) questions may be all you need for this reflection: "What was supposed to happen?" "What really happened?" "What accounts for the difference?" "What will I do differently today?" Alternatively, you may want to consider Martin Seligman's (2011) "PERMA" questions for a flourishing life:

- How **p**ositive was my day?
- How **e**ngaged was I?
- How healthy were my **r**elationships?
- How **m**eaningful were my activities?
- What did I **a**ccomplish?

As with every other aspect of adaptive time management, you'll want to tailor these questions (or choose your own) to create a system that works best for you.

One last thing to consider is the extent to which you hurried through your day. Theologian and University of Southern California philosophy professor Dallas Willard said that we should take it as our aim to live our lives entirely without hurry, which he calls "a state of frantic effort one falls into in response to inadequacy, fear, and guilt" (cited in Comer, 2019, p. xiii).

Fortunately, there are concrete steps we can take to reduce the hurry in our lives. We can build space into our calendar by giving ourselves extra time to reach appointments or complete tasks. We can find some kind of sanctuary where we can unplug and take a mental break. We can adopt a ritual, such as a sabbath or a retreat. We can create no-screen zones in our homes, where phones, tablets, laptops, and video games are not allowed. Perhaps most important, we can develop an effective strategy for saying no. (See William Ury's 2007 book *The Power of a Positive No* for suggestions on how to decline invitations.) When we have the freedom and confidence to say no to others' demands on our time, we can start to have the impact and life we really want to have.

Building Habits

Turning ideas into action is a messy and complex affair that often leads to failure. Too often, there is a huge gap between what we *know* and what we *do*. As Maya Angelou (2018) once beautifully wrote, "Do the best you can until you know better. Then when you know better, do better." The trouble is that, too often, we don't do better, even though we know we should.

One reason we fail to turn ideas into action is that we assume willpower is all we need to change. We buy the gym membership and count on willpower to get us to the gym; then, when our enthusiasm for exercise fizzles out, we blame ourselves for not having the grit to actually do what we know we need do to. But willpower usually isn't enough. If we really want to turn ideas into actions, we need a structure that will ensure that we do what we know we need to do, and that structure is what we call a *habit*. In *The Power of Habit* (2012), Charles Duhigg writes that "a habit is a formula our brain automatically follows... a choice that we deliberately make at some point, and then stop thinking about, but continue doing, often every day" (pp. 284–285). If we keep dropping the ball when it comes to change, the problem is not that we lack grit, but that we lack a structure—a habit.

Contemporary researchers and journalists such as Duhigg, James Clear (2018), Wendy Wood (2019), and B. J. Fogg (2020) have clarified what habits are and why they are so important for leading ourselves. These authors' research will help any coach who wants to adopt new behaviors or support others who choose to change.

Although the researchers use different words to describe how habits work, the descriptions themselves are fairly consistent. A habit begins with a *cue*—some prompt that triggers an action, like a green light in traffic. Next there is a *routine*—a response to the cue or prompt. Finally, there is a *reward* for the action.

Here's an example. I have a habit of drinking coffee each morning. Walking into the kitchen is my cue. The routine is the complicated way I prepare my coffee. The reward is the scent of fresh-ground coffee, the taste of a just-brewed cup, and the pleasant sensation of becoming more awake and alert as I drink.

If a coach wants to develop a habit, a good place to start is to identify the cue. For example, a coach who wants to implement the time management strategies in this chapter might consider the bell at end of the school day as a cue to sit down and plan the next day. After identifying the cue, the coach needs to develop a routine—a simple action or set of actions to do the same way each day. Research (Wood, 2019) suggests that we increase our chances of successfully adopting habits by thinking about how our context enhances or inhibits our ability to form a habit. For example, if you want to engage in time management at the end of the day but find that many teachers want to have a coaching conversation at that time, it's probably best to set aside a different time to implement that habit.

B. J. Fogg (2020) of the Behavior Design Lab at Stanford University suggests keeping things simple when it comes to change. We may be tempted to mix planning our day with many other actions, but the more complex those actions are, the less likely it is that planning will stick as a habit.

For many years, people cited Maxwell Maltz's suggestion in *Psycho-Cybernetics* (1989), first published in 1960, that it takes 21 days to make a habit. Unfortunately, more recent research suggests that it actually takes much longer. Wendy Wood (2019) and her colleagues at the University of Southern California have conducted several studies that suggest the time span is closer to two to three months. If we want to turn an action into a habit, we need to "keep doing it . . . until [we] aren't doing it anymore" (p. 102), Wood writes.

For repetition to work, it's important to do the same action the same way each time. If I want to start the habit of planning my days, it is a good idea to plan at the same time every day. If I sometimes plan in the mornings and other times just before bed, and if I skip some days on top of that, I'm not really repeating the same action, which means I'm not really forming a habit.

Finally, if am going to stick with a habit, it's a lot easier when the new habit is more rewarding than my old way of acting. To develop the habit of reflecting and planning my day, for example, doing those things needs to feel better than not planning. The best rewards are intrinsic. If the act of reflecting and planning is intellectually pleasing, or if at least seeing my plan for each day makes me feel more in control, then I'm more likely to form the habit.

Practicing Self-Care

The strategies for leading yourself hold the potential to help anyone live a more intentional, meaningful life, but there is one thing that can still sabotage our efforts: self-criticism. As Kristin Neff, a researcher at the University of Texas in Austin, has written, "There's almost no one whom we treat as badly as ourselves" (2011, p. 6). To truly lead ourselves, we need to treat ourselves with compassion.

Self-compassion. In her book *Self-Compassion* (2011), Neff explains that we frequently limit our potential by internalizing criticism we've heard from people in our past—a parent, bully, ex-spouse, teacher, coach—and that this leads us to say and think horrible things about ourselves that we would never say to anyone else. A habit of self-criticism coupled with the challenges of doing the complex work of coaching can damage a coach's mental and physical health.

Our self-critical words—"I'm so stupid/undisciplined/weak/fat"—have the same effect on us that they would have if others said them. At its worst, Neff says, self-criticism leads to anxiety, insecurity, depression, and an overall negative attitude toward life. We try to prop up our self-efficacy by comparing ourselves with others, but we know there will always be someone who is faster, thinner, or more accomplished than us. That is why comparison culture is unhealthy for everyone.

The first step in overcoming self-criticism is simply to recognize what we are doing. Just naming examples of self-criticism is a positive step forward. A much healthier response is self-compassion—treating ourselves with the compassion we would direct toward a dear friend. According to Neff, self-compassion involves letting go "of the need to feel better than others" (p. 19), "being kind to ourselves" (p. 41), and "recognizing our shared human condition, flawed and fragile as it is" (p. 10). At its heart, self-compassion is about showing ourselves the same kindness and grace we would show others.

Health. We all want to take care of our health. Too often, though, it feels like trying to be healthy is like trying to read a book of poetry while canoeing through wild rapids on a raging river—reading T. S. Eliot's *Four Quartets* might sound nice, but right now I just need to keep from going over this waterfall.

Most of us have long lists of things we want to do to be healthier. We need to exercise more, eat a healthier diet, drink more water, get more sleep—and we want to do it all tomorrow. Indeed, we would do all these things today, but *other* things keep getting in the way—papers that need to be graded, visiting in-laws, the graduate course, the twins, and that lovely glass of sauvignon blanc we just poured ourselves.

Taking care of our health is one of the most important ways we can lead ourselves, and luckily a few simple adjustments—OK, some are not that simple—can have a very positive impact on our lives, our ability to lead ourselves, and our ability to lead others. But how do we do it? Much of the U.S. national debt could be paid off with the money we've all spent on stationary bikes, treadmills, and gym memberships that never got used once the novelty wore off.

To start eating a healthier diet, exercising, and cutting back on unhealthy habits, we likely need to use the other strategies I've mentioned above. We need to find the motivation to change by acquiring a deeper understanding of why we get up in the morning—our purpose. We need to block time to do whatever is most important. We need to develop habits so that we don't have to rely on our unreliable willpower. Finally, we have to be compassionate toward ourselves, recognizing that we cannot do it all at once, but we *can* take one small step forward at a time to lead ourselves more effectively. And the more effectively we lead ourselves, the more effectively we will lead others.

Leading Others

When I did a Google search on leadership in August 2020, my search turned up more than 2,760,000,000 results. Such a staggering figure means at least two things. First, leadership is very important. Second, you've likely read about and applied a lot of key leadership concepts yourself.

According to the literature, effective leaders are emotionally intelligent, good at using their relationship-building skills to bring teams of people together around shared goals. They are great listeners, and they genuinely care about their employees. Their ego is not as important as the larger purpose that drives their actions. They understand organizational culture and treat each person uniquely. And they aren't hypocrites—effective leaders walk the talk.

Like all leaders, coaches are most effective when they demonstrate these leadership strategies. A lot can be learned from authors like Michael Fullan, Chimamanda Ngozi Adichie, Brené Brown, and Pedro Noguera. But four leadership strategies are especially important for coaches, particularly when they work from the Partnership Principles:

1. Balancing ambition with humility
2. Being a Multiplier
3. Creating alignment
4. Making good decisions

Balancing Ambition with Humility

In the past, I've profiled various coaches and their successful and unsuccessful approaches to leading. In *Unmistakable Impact* (2011), for example, I wrote about two coaches I named John LeClair and Lauren Morgan, who were less successful than they had hoped. John did everything he could think of to push his teachers to act but found that "the more he pushed his colleagues, the less enthusiastic they became" (p. 125). In contrast to John, Lauren refused to force herself onto teachers, preferring to stay in the background. She only worked with teachers who came to her for help: "She waited patiently, but the right time never seemed to come along" (p. 125). In the end, Lauren had no more impact than John did.

In *Instructional Coaching* (Knight, 2007), I describe Jean Clark, who experienced more success than John and Lauren did. Jean "took a partnership approach with her teachers, but at the same time... was willful, deliberate, and driven as she led change at her school" (p. 212). Jean's efforts produced such significant gains in student achievement that her principal, Joe Buckley, called me at the end of the school year just to read me the school's test scores and to praise Jean.

Looking back at these three coaches, we see that John failed because, although he was ambitious, he was not responsive to teachers. Lauren failed for the opposite reason—though she was responsive, she was not ambitious. Jean succeeded because she was able to strike the right balance between ambition and responsiveness.

I first heard about balancing ambition and humility in Jim Collins's now legendary book *Good to Great* (2001). Collins compared "good" companies with "great" ones, finding that leaders in the latter are (1) capable people who (2) work well with teams, (3) manage people and resources effectively, (4) unite and motivate people to achieve a compelling vision, and (5) "embody a paradoxical mix of personal humility and professional will" (p. 39).

After *Good to Great,* Collins wrote *Good to Great and the Social Sectors* (2005), about leadership in organizations like schools. The most effective leaders, Collins writes, "are ambitious first and foremost for the cause, the movement, the mission, the work—not themselves—and they have the will to do whatever it takes… to make good on this ambition." A leader's "compelling combination of personal humility and professional will," he continues, "is a key factor in creating legitimacy and influence" (p. 11).

Based on my own experience, coaches need to balance ambition and humility just as much as CEOs of corporations do, and they demonstrate their ambition for change by using many of the strategies described in this chapter so far. They know their purpose, and they focus on doing what is necessary to ensure that all students flourish. They develop habits and use their time effectively to foster trust and make sure the most important work gets done. They take care of themselves so that they can do the challenging and incredibly important work of leading change in schools. Because they are organized, reliable, and ambitious for the greater good, they keep everyone's focus on what matters, refusing to accept leaving anyone behind.

At the same time, coaches demonstrate humility by keeping their focus on what's best for children, not what's best for themselves. As instructional coach Angela Kolb told us, "Leadership means doing what is best for kids and staff even if it isn't what is best for you. Leadership is about relationships and is not about ego." Truly, when a person takes in the full complexity of teaching and sees how challenging it is to teach, a humble response is the only appropriate one. Coaches demonstrate their humility by becoming excellent listeners and engaging their will to do what is truly best for teachers and students. Effective coaches listen, learn, and respond in ways that honor teachers' professional autonomy.

Both humility and ambition can be challenging for anyone to keep in check. We might be tempted to say things like "I'm not a good questioner" or

"I'm not very organized, so I can't be reliable." But the positions we choose compel us to become the people we need to be to do the work we need to do. Just as we wouldn't want an airplane mechanic to say, "I'm not really a details person," teachers don't want a coach to say, "I'm just not much of a listener."

Being a Multiplier

Researchers Liz Wiseman and Greg McKeown set out to discover better effective leadership by studying 150 leaders in 35 companies on 4 continents. Their most important conclusion, described in their book *Multipliers* (2010), is that some leaders increase the intelligence, energy, and capabilities of those around them, ultimately guiding their employees to be two or three times more effective than they used to be. The authors label these leaders as *Multipliers*. Other leaders do the opposite: they decrease people's confidence, energy, motivation, and self-efficacy. The authors label these leaders as *Diminishers*. The best coaches are Multipliers; the worst are Diminishers.

When we introduce the concepts of Multipliers and Diminishers in our workshops at the Instructional Coaching Group, participants can usually describe people they've known who fall into both categories. Multipliers are listeners—they see the strengths in others, are open to others' ideas, and act in ways that show they are focused on the needs and interests of others. Diminishers, in contrast, do most of the talking, see people's weaknesses more than their strengths, shoot down others' ideas, and keep the focus on themselves.

Wiseman and McKeown identify several characteristics of Multipliers and Diminishers, three of which seem especially relevant to coaches as leaders. Multipliers are *Talent Finders, Liberators,* and *Challengers.*

Talent Finders. Multipliers, suggest Wiseman and McKeown, see the talents in others even when others don't see those talents in themselves and help them become more aware of their strengths. They acknowledge that different people have different strengths and weaknesses, but they believe everyone can improve. Simply put, Multipliers embrace what Carol Dweck (2007) refers to as a growth mindset. Wiseman and McKeown found that Multipliers have a knack for finding other people's native genius—"something more specific than a strength... that people do not only exceptionally well, but absolutely naturally" (p. 30).

Coaches who are Talent Finders carefully observe those with whom they work to identify their native genius and communicate it to others. As Wiseman and McKeown explain, "If people aren't aware of their genius, they are not in a position to deliberately utilize it. By telling people what you see you can raise their awareness and confidence, allowing them to provide their capability more fully" (p. 32).

Liberators. Even when people become aware of their strengths, they may encounter obstacles that keep them from flourishing. "Multipliers liberate people from the too-often oppressive forces within institutional hierarchy," write Wiseman and McKeown. "They liberate people to think, to speak, and to act with reason. They give people permission to think" (p. 47).

Coaches who are Liberators can promote learning by building psychologically safe learning partnerships that free teachers to experiment, take risks, iterate, and use a coaching cycle such as the Impact Cycle.

Challengers. Multipliers challenge people to improve. By contrast, Wiseman and McKeown write, "know-it-alls" hold others back in order to maintain their expert status. "At the core of the Challenger's logic is the belief that people grow through challenge and, hence, want to be stretched" (p. 72).

Coaches and other leaders can challenge others by offering questions instead of answers. A good question puts the ball in the collaborating teachers' court, positioning them as the decision makers, and powerful questions often generate new insights.

Effective instructional coaching is structured to create the very kind of challenge Wiseman and McKeown describe. Teachers, in partnership with coaches, get a clear picture of reality and set a goal, with the gap between where they are now and where they want to be creating an essential creative tension (more on this later in this chapter).

The Accidental Diminisher. Even with the best intentions, we can become what Wiseman and McKeown refer to as Accidental Diminishers. For example, we might offer so many ideas that we silence collaborating teachers, or we might always be "on," projecting so much energy that we exhaust those around us. We can also be Accidental Diminishers by stepping in to rescue people whenever we see them struggle (inadvertently creating dependency or resentment), or when we push people to move forward at too accelerated a pace. We can even be Accidental Diminishers by being too optimistic, glossing over challenges and assuming that every problem can be solved with hard work.

To determine whether you are an Accidental Diminisher, show a trusted advisor a video of a coaching session and ask for feedback. "Leading like a Multiplier," write Wiseman and McKeown, "is a choice we encounter daily or perhaps in every moment… a single Accidental Diminisher turned Multiplier could have a profound and far-reaching impact in a world where the challenges are so great and our full intelligence underutilized" (p. 166).

Creating Alignment

Coaches who take the partnership approach do not see their job as one of motivating teachers to do what they, in their role as coaches, have determined teachers should do. Rather, they see their work as supporting teachers as they set goals. I call this "coaching in alignment."

Coaching in alignment embodies the principle of equality. When a coach and a teacher are in alignment, the teacher has as much power as the coach. The teacher and coach are fully invested in work that they both believe is important for the teacher (and, especially, for student learning). Coaching in alignment is never imposed on a teacher; it is truly an act of service for both coaches and teachers.

The Partnership Principles help establish alignment between coaches and teachers. When coaches have an authentic, humble desire to learn from teachers, see and affirm teachers' strengths, and demonstrate that they truly have teachers' best interest at heart, teachers are more likely to engage fully in coaching. Additionally, coaches who ask powerful questions and genuinely listen will better understand teachers' goals, needs, and concerns.

Alignment and motivation. Of course, alignment isn't possible if the teacher isn't interested in collaborating in the first place. But coaching is not about motivating others or overcoming their resistance. That is, the question is not, as Deci and Flaste (2013) remind us, "how can people motivate others" but, rather, "how can people create the conditions within which others will motivate themselves" (p. 10).

In my workshops, I often ask participants to describe times when they have been truly motivated to make positive changes. They almost always report that they are motivated either because they are experiencing a problem and want to get better (e.g., they're motivated to cut out junk food because they are unhappy with their level of health) or because they have a positive vision of what they could be (e.g., they're motivated to create highly engaging learning experiences because they have a positive vision of their students in love with learning). Sometimes people are motivated by both these factors at the same time.

When coaches work in alignment with teachers, they help them get a clearer picture of their current reality and set an attractive goal so that they can see the discrepancy between the two for themselves. Coaches don't tell teachers what to do, but provide opportunities for teachers to realize what they really want to do, and through the entire process they ensure that teachers are the decision makers. As instructional coach Lorrie Cariaga says, "Leaders help people see potential within themselves."

Making Good Decisions

To establish and maintain alignment with others, coaches must make good decisions, which will in turn lead to better coaching. Nobel laureate Daniel Kahneman's (2011) insights into decision making illuminate the complex nature of thinking while coaching. Kahneman contends that decisions usually involve two completely different cognitive processes: *thinking fast* and *thinking slow*. Thinking fast refers to decisions we make so quickly that we don't even consciously pay attention to them, whereas thinking slow refers to decisions we are able to think about beforehand. Hitting the brakes when a car cuts in front of us is thinking fast; deciding whether to sue the other driver after the accident is thinking slow. Both ways of making decisions are important, and both are a part of every coach's life.

Thinking slow

Many of the decisions that coaches make involve thinking slow—deciding whether to raise an issue with the principal, or to keep working with uncooperative teachers, or, indeed, to keep coaching at all. Fortunately, a body of knowledge has emerged to help us make sound, careful decisions over time.

Step 1: Identify options. A good first step toward making better decisions involves moving away from binary (yes/no) thinking by seeking as wide a variety of options as possible. To this end, Stephen Johnson (2018) suggests talking with people of different genders, races, sexual orientations, ages, perspectives, and so on. Diverse teams are smarter teams.

We can also surface more options by discussing our situation with people outside our immediate group: experts, people who have succeeded where others have struggled, people who have given good suggestions in the past. Additionally, we can try to imagine what we would do if none of our current options were available. For example, a coach and teacher who are trying to identify the best strategy for hitting a goal might ask, "If we don't use any of the strategies we've discussed, what else might we use?"

Step 2: Make predictions. After we have expanded our options, we need to predict which of them will prove to be best. This usually starts with gathering information (through internet searches, formal interviews, or informal conversations). Former Secretary of State Colin Powell suggests that in order to make good decisions, we need to have between 40 and 70 percent of available information at our disposal (cited in Harrari, 2002).

Many also find it helpful to list all their assumptions before trying to make a decision. Chip and Dan Heath (2013) suggest we ask ourselves the question "What can I reasonably expect to happen if I make this choice?" (p. 121). For her part, Suzy Welch (2009) developed the 10-10-10 rule, which prompts us to ask, "How will this decision affect my life in 10 minutes, in 10 months, and in 10 years?" Still another approach, promoted by psychologist Gary Klein (2007), is to hold a mental "premortem" by asking, "Let's assume the patient dies. What will it be that kills him?"

Step 3: Making the decision by reducing options. Eventually, we have to make a decision, and we usually do that by eliminating any options that don't seem relevant. If we get lost in the details, we may end up with choice paralysis, so removing all the options we are certain we won't choose can be very helpful.

For centuries, people have been making decisions by creating lists of pros and cons. In his book *Farsighted* (2018), Steven Johnson explains that Charles Darwin even created one to decide whether to get married. On the "Not Marry" side of his list, Darwin included such items as "Less money for books" (p. 8). On the "Marry" side, he wrote "Constant companion (and friend in old age)." Darwin was married six months after he created the list.

The problem with a simple pros-and-cons list is that not all pros and cons are created equal. Darwin probably understood that a lifelong loving companion is more valuable than having a surplus of money for books. Jeff Bezos, founder and president of Amazon, uses a simple criterion to make a decision: if he is 70 percent certain of a positive outcome, he acts (Bezos, 2016).

I have made a lot of decisions based on two simple criteria: what is easiest and what is most powerful. When choosing a teaching strategy for the classroom, for example, I want to know which one will be easiest for the teacher to implement and which one will have the most positive impact on students' lives. If it's both powerful and easy, I've found, it's usually a winning option.

Chip and Dan Heath (2013) recommend that people make decisions only after they clarify their principles or core priorities. A coach who knows that one of his or her core principles is to do what is best for children, for example, will find it easier to navigate many complex decisions.

Thinking fast

Much as it can be nice to have the luxury of time when making decisions, coaches need to think fast almost every time they interact with collaborating teachers. In a flash, they need to read teachers' facial expressions and body language, assess whether teachers feel safe in a conversation, choose which questions to ask, and decide when to move back and forth between facilitative and dialogical approaches to interaction.

One aspect of thinking fast is to apply the coaching skill of noticing. In particular, coaches need to notice the nonverbal communication of their collaborating teacher (see also p. 47). Does the teacher's tone of voice sound enthusiastic? Does she sit up straighter when she talks about certain topics? Does she make appropriate eye contact? Is she energized? Does she respond enthusiastically to questions or hesitate for a half-second before responding? In short, the coach should always be assessing whether the teacher feels safe, is open, and is focused on a goal that matters.

Additionally, coaches need to be self-aware. Do they feel at ease in the conversation? Do they feel the teacher is open and candid? Are they energized about partnering with the teacher to meet the identified goal? Do they feel positively about the conversation? Do they feel that their emotions are under control?

If coaches determine that they are out of alignment with the collaborating teacher, the first thing they ought to do is take a step back and listen. Once a coach fully understands the teacher's needs and emotions, he can start to partner with the teacher to identify a powerful goal that she really wants to pursue.

Many coaches use single phrases, often referred to as *mantras,* to help them make better decisions when they have to think fast. Author, consultant, and coach Michelle Harris, for example, has found Susan Scott's (2002) phrase "respect the sweet purity of silence" to be an incredibly helpful mantra. "I say that mantra to myself over and over and over again in my head," she said. "And to be quite honest, I also have to literally bite my tongue to honor silence." Christian van Nieuwerburgh (2017) uses the mantra "It's not about me" to help him resist the temptation to solve another person's problem. Ann Hoffman shares Michael Bungay Stanier's mantra "Be more curious" (2020) when she leads workshops on my book *Better Conversations* (Knight, 2015). These mantras all provide those who use them with a foundation for making better decisions when things are moving quickly.

Other Coaching Mantras
Don't take sides. (William Miller and Stephen Rollnick)
Put the teacher in the driver's seat. (Ann Hoffman)
Let the other person sit in the big chair. (Dan Pink)
Do the right thing. (Spike Lee)
Let the teacher make the decisions.
Let go of control.

Everyday decision making. When I talk with people about how they make decisions, very few of them describe a step-by-step process. Most people make decisions informally in the moments and days of their lives, but that doesn't make the strategies they use any less powerful. In the moment, coaches can think carefully about their principles, consider the 10-10-10 rule, go to a wise friend for advice, or remind themselves that "it's not about me."

Good decision making usually isn't a linear or academic process, but it *can* be strategic, leading to better outcomes.

To Sum Up

This chapter describes strategies for leading yourself and leading others.

We need to lead ourselves because it is difficult to be a force for good if we burn out. To lead ourselves, I suggest that we clarify our purpose, develop a personalized approach to managing our time, develop positive habits, and take care of ourselves through self-compassion.

We need to lead others because life is short, and we want our days, weeks, and years to count for something important. To lead others, we should balance ambition with humility, be Multipliers, create alignment, and make good decisions.

Reflection Questions

Leading Yourself

1. Is your work energizing? Are you living out your life's purpose? If not, what is one thing you can do to move closer to a purposeful life?
2. On a scale of 1 to 10, how well are you managing your time? Is there anything you should change to manage your time more effectively?
3. Are there any good habits you want to adopt or bad habits you want to give up? Can you use the ideas about habits in this chapter to change your behavior in any way?
4. Are you taking care of yourself? Do you treat yourself with the same compassion you show to others? If not, why not, and when will you start to demonstrate self-compassion? Is there anything else you need to do to take care of yourself?

Leading Others

1. How effectively do you balance ambition and humility? Should you do more to set up conditions for change to happen? Do you need to be more responsive to teachers?
2. Are you an Accidental Diminisher? What evidence do you have to support your thinking? Is there anything you can do to be more of a Multiplier?

3. How often do you feel you are in alignment with the teachers you coach? Is there anything you or others need to change to increase the alignment between coaches and teachers?

4. How effectively do you think fast and slow? Are there any coaching mantras that you would like to adopt? Do you want to change anything else about how you make decisions?

Going Deeper

This chapter was a bear to write. I looked at more than 75 books and struggled to summarize all that I learned from those authors, the 100-plus coaches ICG researcher Geoff Knight and I surveyed, and the two dozen coaches Geoff and I interviewed. But the struggle has been worth it. I've been shaped by the process of writing this chapter, and this means that there are a lot of resources you could read to deepen your understanding of the leadership ideas in this book.

- If you want to read more about purpose and the Japanese concept of *ikigai*, I recommend Héctor García and Francesc Miralles's *Ikigai* (2016). I found the book to be inspiring, entertaining, and practical, and I applied the ideas right away.

- The classic work on time management is David Allen's *Getting Things Done* (2015). People follow the GTD methodology with the same enthusiasm Deadheads show for the Grateful Dead, and anyone interested in organizing their lives will benefit from reading the book. Allen's ideas don't always fit my personal style, but I'm convinced anyone can learn a great deal from them.

- Recently, there has been a proliferation of books on habits, influenced most likely by Charles Duhigg's *The Power of Habit* (2012). I personally found Wendy Wood's book *Good Habits, Bad Habits* (2019) to be especially helpful because, along with providing practical tips on how to develop good habits, Wood includes the evidence to support her claims.

- If you are going to read just one book on taking care of yourself, I recommend Kristin Neff's *Self-Compassion* (2011). Her primary message, that we should give ourselves the same compassion we would extend to a friend, is an important one for everyone to hear.

- I've read a number of excellent books on decision making, and Chip and Dan Heath's *Decisive* (2013) stands out for being entertaining, accessible, and practical (just like all their other books). In fact, I've used the book as my guide to making some important personal decisions.
- I recommend Wiseman, Allen, and Foster's book *The Multiplier Effect* (2013) because they apply research about Multipliers to schools. Their research has helped me better understand what I need to do to be an effective leader.
- Finally, the classic book on motivation and change is Miller and Rollnick's *Motivational Interviewing* (2013), which has profoundly shaped the way I understand coaching.

What's Next?

There are many suggestions for change in this chapter, but you should start by implementing no more than one or two of them. For example, you might want to implement the ideas about habits to make a change in your health or personal development, or you might want to use the strategies described to create more aligned interactions with teachers.

One way to identify what to do is to review your answers to the reflection questions above and make a list of all the things you could change. Once you've made your list, apply the criteria I suggest in this chapter to identify your next steps. Ask yourself, "What is the one thing I see on my list that both is easy and has a high potential to have a positive outcome?"

What You Do

Learning Map for Chapter 4

The Impact Cycle

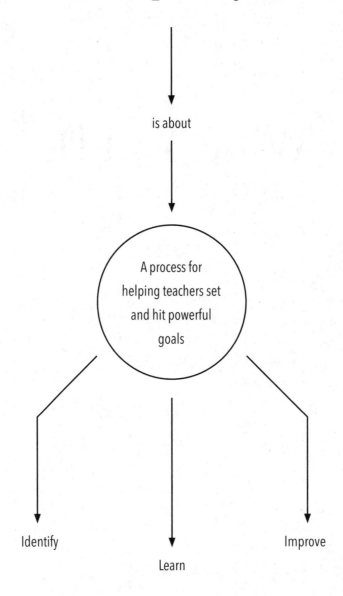

is about

A process for helping teachers set and hit powerful goals

Identify

Learn

Improve

4 The Impact Cycle

You are never too old to set another goal or to dream a new dream.

—C. S. Lewis

In January 2019, Leigh Anstadt came to an ICG institute with two of her colleagues. Leigh was going to oversee the elementary instructional coaching program in Utah's Canyons School District and rightly felt she should experience the same professional development as her coaches. At the end of the institute, Leigh decided that she needed to complete her own Impact Cycle. In short, she needed to be a coach if she was going to lead the coaches.

Leigh asked Angela Haycock to be her "guinea pig." Angela was a 5th grade teacher who came to the profession later in life. "My mom was a teacher, her mom was a teacher, and I knew that someday I wanted to be a teacher, too," she said. "Getting hired by Canyons School District was probably one of the best things for me." As this story will reveal, Canyons was also fortunate to have Angela work for them.

"Angela was fabulous," Leigh said. "People tell you she is a great teacher. You go into her classroom and you can feel it. The kids love her." Angela told us she was very busy and "a little apprehensive about coaching, but I try to push myself, and I knew coaching would probably be a good thing for me to do, so I thought, 'Let's do it.'"

With Angela's permission, Leigh recorded every coaching conversation she had. "I forced myself to watch every session and reflect on my coaching," Leigh said. "I wanted to review the conversations so I could hear myself talking or not talking, asking not telling, and reflect on my coaching. I decided I needed to live the Impact Cycle and experience it—walk it rather than just talk it."

The Impact Cycle starts with the Identify stage, during which the collaborating teacher, in partnership with the coach, identifies a clear picture of reality, a goal, and a strategy to hit the goal. Angela chose to focus on achievement. In Canyons School District, a major assessment is the District-Wide Standards Based Assessment (DWSBA), which is given four times a year. When Leigh met with Angela to talk about getting a clear picture of reality, Angela had just received her DWSBA results, which showed that only 12 out of 30 students had gotten the top score of 3 or 4. This provided a clear indication that although students were enjoying class, many were not learning what they needed to learn. Consequently, state assessment data became the main way Angela and Leigh established a clear picture of reality.

Leigh partnered with Angela to set a goal for improvement by drawing from a list of Identify questions (see p. 93). "I tried hard to be intentional about sticking to asking questions, listening, and letting her guide the ship because I really wanted her to do the work so it would be her victory," Leigh said.

At first, Leigh noticed Angela gave the same answer to every question: "I don't know." But Leigh refused to give Angela advice. "I realized that if you wait long enough, people usually come up with an answer," said Leigh. "I think Angela's self-efficacy improved because she came up with the answers, said them out loud, and then got positive feedback."

Angela told us much the same thing. "Leigh was constantly telling me that it was my class and that I knew what would work best," she said. "She did a great job of asking questions but then leaving them open for me to figure out where to go next. I think my confidence was built because I could figure out, 'Hey, I've got this; I can do this.'"

When Leigh asked the Identify questions, Angela quickly came up with the goal that 25 out of 30 students would hit proficiency on the next test. Leigh and Angela checked the goal to make sure it was powerful, easy, emotionally compelling, reachable, and student-focused (i.e., a PEERS goal; see pp. 91–92). "The goal was the pin, or the anchor—the center point of the whole thing," said Leigh.

Leigh came to coaching conversations with a lot of knowledge about effective instruction. She had attended many workshops on John Hattie's *Visible Learning* (2008) and knew how important teacher clarity, success criteria, formative assessment, and feedback were to Hattie. So when she met with Angela, she shared those ideas while also making sure that Angela came up with the specific teaching strategies she wanted to use to help her students move closer to the goal.

"Leigh guided the discussions to a certain point, and then she would leave it for me to think about and look deeper," Angela recounted. "Leigh would never say 'Here, let me give you an answer' or 'Here, let's try this, let's do this,' which was great. She was suggesting a direction, but then letting me figure it out."

Angela decided that her students would do a close reading of the DWSBA rubric and then complete formative assessments so they could monitor their progress toward the goal. Leigh helped Angela clarify exactly how to implement those strategies. Then she partnered with her to make modifications when the assessments suggested that students weren't learning (i.e., the Learn and Improve stages of the Impact Cycle).

Leigh met with Angela on the day the DWSBA results were released. "When I walked in, Angela announced, 'We made it!'" she said. "She was really excited and so anxious to share, and so proud of her students for what they did. She said, 'Look at this one, look what they did,' celebrating their work. It wasn't about her at all."

Angela was still enthusiastic about the results when we interviewed her. "When the students hit the goal, it felt fantastic," she said. "I wanted the kids to feel successful in their writing skills because I knew that going into middle school and high school, writing is what a lot of teachers focus on. I wanted to be here for those kids, and I wanted them to feel success. So it was a satisfying feeling to know 'Hey, I helped these kids.'"

For Leigh, the change in students validated the entire cycle. The long-term impact was that students were excited about writing. In Leigh's words, "Once the students understood that they had power and control over their writing and a clear vision of the target, they loved it. Their love of writing really caught fire, and it oozed out into other areas all day. When kids are excited about stuff, it carries over."

The Impact Cycle

The Impact Cycle that Leigh used brings the Partnership Principles to life. Done well, the cycle leads to powerful results. It involves easy-to-learn stages and steps that coaches can master and implement quickly.

Pre-Cycle Conversation

Like most things in life, coaching is most likely to succeed when it gets off to a good start. For this reason, the coach should have a short conversation with the collaborating teacher before they dive into the coaching cycle.

First impressions shape all future impressions, so during this conversation, the coach should listen with empathy, affirm rather than judge, and communicate that she believes in the teacher and truly wants what's best for him. The coach should start by encouraging the teacher to discuss any concerns or questions he may have. After addressing these, the coach should summarize the stages of the Impact Cycle, explain the confidentiality policy, and clarify that the teacher decides on his own what to implement in his classroom. The coach should explain that she is there to help the teacher achieve his goals, not to impose her own ideas on the teacher. Throughout the pre-cycle conversation, the coach should frequently ask the teacher if he has any questions.

Next, the coach should explain the Impact Cycle in greater detail by going through each item on a checklist summarizing it. She should explain each action on the list, confirm that the teacher understands it, and then ask if the teacher wants to do the action as described or modify it in some way. To be able to explain the cycle clearly, the coach needs to have a deep understanding of each of its stages and steps.

Identify
- Teacher gets a clear picture of current reality by watching a video of his lesson or by reviewing observation data (video is best).
- Teacher works with coach to answer the Identify questions and identify a student-focused goal.
- Teacher identifies a teaching strategy to use to hit the goal.

Learn
- Coach shares a checklist for the chosen teaching strategy.
- Coach prompts teacher to modify the practice if teacher wishes.
- Teacher chooses an approach to modeling that he would like to observe and identifies a time to watch modeling.
- Coach provides modeling in one or more formats.
- Teacher sets a time to implement the practice.

Improve
- Teacher implements the practice.
- Teacher or coach gathers data (in class or while viewing video) on student progress toward to the goal.
- Teacher or coach gathers data (in class or while viewing video) on teacher's implementation of the practice (usually on the previously viewed checklist).
- Teacher and coach meet to confirm direction and monitor progress.
- Teacher and coach make adaptations and plan next actions until the goal is met.

After the teacher has reviewed the checklist and received answers to all his questions, the coach and teacher should make a plan for the next six weeks, identifying when each of the steps of the cycle will occur. I think it is best if the coach and teacher determine the exact dates when each activity will occur. As Denise Brennan-Nelson (2005) has written, "'Someday' is not a day of the week."

Lastly, after the meeting, the coach should send a detailed email to the collaborating teacher restating key ideas (for example, about confidentiality and decision making) and listing all the cycle steps and when she hopes to complete them.

Stage One: Identify

Step 1: Identifying a clear picture of reality

When we choose to change, we often do it because we see a big difference between where we are and where we want to be (Miller & Rollnick, 2013). Consequently, our motivation takes a hit when we don't see reality clearly. The interviews my colleagues and I have done with teachers, coaches, and administrators (Knight, 2014) show that educators, just like most other professionals, don't have a clear picture of what they do. Teachers need to have a clear picture of reality, or they almost certainly won't see the need to change.

Most of us struggle to clearly see what we do because of perceptual errors. *Confirmation bias,* for example, is the tendency to consciously or unconsciously seek out data that reinforce our assumptions. People "tend to see what they expect to see" (Grant-Halvorson, 2015, p. 23). *Attribution error* describes a habit of blaming others for our missteps but excusing ourselves for the same mistakes. *Stereotyping* occurs when we overgeneralize the characteristics of people in a group, whereas *primacy effect* refers to our bias toward overgeneralizing our first experiences with a person. *Halo effect* describes our tendency to assume that a person has many positive characteristics after seeing them exhibit just one positive characteristic. Last, *habituation* comes from our tendency to stop noticing the unique features of something we experience all the time (e.g., seeing the same students every day, a teacher may stop noticing some of the unique features of learning or behavior that they exhibit in the classroom).

A second major reason we don't see reality clearly is that we use defense mechanisms as a kind of shield from unpleasant realities. Given the emotional complexity of life, some defense mechanisms are necessary; life would simply be too difficult without them. As Prochaska, DiClemente, and Norcross (1994) have written, "Without the protection of these 'mental shields' we would be bombarded constantly by undesirable feelings and external threats, both real and imagined. Defensive reactions allow us to avoid, temporarily at least, what we cannot confront, and let us get on with our lives" (p. 82).

While defensiveness can protect our emotional state, it keeps us from changing in ways that might in fact lead us to more success or even better lives. Being aware of defense mechanisms can help us figure out the best approach to change with others. As shown in Figure 4.1, Prochaska and colleagues (1994) identify several defense mechanisms.

Since a clear picture of reality is important for motivation and to ensure we are focused on an important issue, it is important to cut through the biases and see reality for what it is. I have identified four ways in which coaches can help teachers do this: (1) video-recording so teachers can watch their lessons, (2) interviewing students, (3) reviewing student work, and (4) gathering observation data.

FIGURE 4.1	
Common Defense Mechanisms	
Defense Mechanism	**Definition**
Denial and minimization	Choosing not to see unpleasant data
Rationalization	Justifying our behavior even if our justifications are irrational
Blaming others	Excusing our situation by blaming or scapegoating others
Blaming ourselves	Failing to acknowledge reality by blaming ourselves for unpleasant occurrences

Video. Studies conducted on micro-teaching and video at Stanford University as far back as the 1960s demonstrated that video accelerates professional learning (Allen, Cooper, & Fortune, 1967). However, before Steve Jobs introduced the iPhone, the cameras needed for recording a lesson were far too cumbersome and distracting for regular classrooms. Now it is very easy for teachers to record their lessons, and more and more teachers are doing what athletes have done for decades: recording themselves doing their work so they can see how to get better.

When using video, coaches need to ensure that teachers feel psychologically safe by explaining that any video recordings are owned by the teacher and that no one will look at them unless the teacher chooses to share them. Coaches should explain that there are many ways they can gather video recordings of lessons: they can record students and keep the teacher out of the video, record video on the teacher's phone, or do a model lesson and have the teacher record the lesson just to see what video looks like.

We have found that teachers learn more when they watch the video separately from their coaches, then come together later to discuss what they saw. Teachers also get more out of watching their video if they use forms (such as the "Student" and "Teacher" forms that can be downloaded at www .instructionalcoaching.com/bookstore/the-definitive-guide-to-instructional-coaching) to analyze their video before meeting their coach. (My book *Focus on Teaching: Using Video for High-Impact Instruction* [Knight, 2014] contains a lot more information about how to use video to help teachers get a clear picture of reality.)

Interviews. Another way to get a clear picture of reality involves interviewing students. Interviews can uncover how students are responding to content, their emotional engagement or physical or psychological safety, whether they feel they belong in the class or their school, or whether they expect to succeed. Below are some examples of questions coaches could ask, but they should feel free to partner with teachers to come up with a list of questions that specifically address the teachers' most pressing concerns.

Questions for Student Interviews
- How would you describe the class to a friend?
- How do your friends describe this class?
- What do you like best about this class?
- What do you enjoy about coming to this class?
- How do you feel about other students in the class?
- If you were the teacher, how would you change this class?
- What does a really good day in class look like for you? What does a really bad day look like?
- Is this class too hard, too easy, or just right?
- What do you wish your teacher did more often? Less often?
- How confident are you that you will pass this class?

One-to-one conversations are best. Interviews can occur in a nearby empty classroom, in the hall, or at the back of class in classrooms where a quiet conversation will not be distracting. The coach should prompt the teacher to select a broad sample of students, including extroverts and introverts, students from different cultures, students who are learning English, students with disabilities, and students who are succeeding and not succeeding. The coach should take detailed notes to share with the collaborating teacher when they meet to set a goal.

Student work. Student learning also provides an important way to clarify classroom reality. Student work, standardized test scores, selected-response or short-answer tests, rubrics, and checks for understanding (I say a lot more about these measures in Chapter 5) all help paint pictures of classroom reality. Sometimes the coach and teacher simply need to have an informal conversation to clarify how students are performing.

Observation of the class. Coaches can also gather data on teaching strategies and student learning using some kind of observation form (e.g., the district evaluation tool suggested in Charlotte Danielson's 2007 book *Enhancing Professional Practice: A Framework for Teaching*)—but cautiously, and only if it is requested by the teacher. Since most professionals, including teachers, don't begin with a clear picture of reality, conversations about the observation data can be awkward. Often, the teacher quite literally does not see what an observer sees. Additionally, data gathered by observers are usually not as objective and valid as the observers might think (Buckingham & Goodall, 2019). A better option is for the coach to video-record a lesson and the teacher to use the evaluation form to assess her own lesson.

Mixed methods. There is rarely enough time to do everything, but teachers and coaches will get a clearer picture of reality when the coach uses more than one method. For example, if a coach and teacher only look at student achievement, they will miss important data, such as how many students are engaged or how much time is spent on transitions. The teacher and coach would see a lot more if they combined looking at student work and video, for example. What matters is that the teacher goes beyond perceptual errors to see the class for what it is. Once a teacher has a clear picture of reality, the teacher and coach can meet to identify a goal.

Step 2: Identify a goal (part 1): PEERS goals

When I studied goal setting with coaches from Beaverton, Oregon, we started with SMART goals (i.e., goals that are *specific, measurable, achievable, relevant,* and *time-bound*) but found that they missed some important elements. After reading the literature and trying out different models, we arrived at what I refer to as "PEERS goals"—goals that are *powerful, easy, emotionally compelling, reachable,* and *student-focused.* If your district expects teachers to set SMART goals, you don't need to throw them out, but our research suggests you'll have more success if those goals meet the PEERS criteria, too.

Powerful. These are goals that make a socially significant difference in students' lives. Simply put, students' lives are unmistakably better after a PEERS goal has been met.

Easy. Any powerful goal to be met in a classroom is going to involve challenges, so the coach and teacher need to identify the easiest way to go about meeting it. A powerful goal that is too difficult to implement won't have any impact on student learning or well-being. Remember: the most direct path to the goal is often the best path.

Emotionally compelling. Effective goals address issues that are important both to the collaborating teacher and to the affected students. As Heath and Heath (2010) have written, the best goal is not "just big and compelling; it should hit you in the gut" (p. 76). When teachers identify goals that really matter to them, their passion drives the process forward. The job of coaches is to then support the teachers' work.

Reachable. Effective goals are measurable. They clarify what will be different after a goal is met. Additionally, a teacher with a reachable goal is able to identify a strategy that can be used to hit the goal. When teachers know exactly what their goals are and how to meet them, they have a reachable goal.

Student-focused. A student-focused goal, such as "Ninety percent of students can consistently write well-organized paragraphs as measured by a single-factor rubric" or "Eighty-five percent of students are cognitively engaged in class," provides an objective standard for measuring how well a teaching strategy is working out in a teacher's classroom. Usually, to hit a goal, the teacher has to implement a strategy effectively, and the strategy has to be sufficiently powerful. If the strategy is implemented successfully but doesn't help students meet their goals, it isn't working. We have also found that teachers are more likely to keep using a strategy when the goal focuses on student improvement rather than strategy implementation.

PEERS goals might have been the most important concept that Leigh Anstadt learned at ICG's institute. "The thing that our coaching was missing was having a finish line—having an end to that cycle," she said. "That was a defining point for me." She added that PEERS goals "became the center of every conversation, the measuring stick we used to close the gap between current reality and the goal. That's why [participating in the institute] was so important. PEERS goals changed everything."

Step 2: Identify a goal (part 2): Identify questions

During the last decade, we have created and refined a list of questions that coaches can use to help teachers set PEERS goals. The questions, listed below, are not to be used the same way every time; in fact, we expect that every coaching conversation will be different. Coaching, like listening, is more like improvising than following a recipe.

The Core Identify Questions
- What's on your mind?
- On a scale of 1 to 10, with 1 being the worst lesson you've taught and 10 being the best, how would you rank the lesson?
- Why did you give it that number?
- What would have to change to move the lesson closer to a 10?
- What would your students be doing differently if your class were a 10?
- In greater detail, what would that look like?
- How could you measure that change?
- Do you want that to be your goal?
- If you could meet that goal, would it really matter to you?

Coaches need to avoid leading questions and instead ask questions that prompt the teacher to think creatively.

More Questions
- If you woke up tomorrow and a miracle happened so that your students were doing exactly what you would like them to do, what would be different? What would be the first signs that the miracle occurred? (Jackson & Waldman)
- What pleased you? (John Campbell)
- And what else? (Michael Bungay Stanier)
- If this class were your dream class, what would be different?

Step 3: Identify a strategy

Right after setting a goal, the teacher needs to identify the best path for meeting it. At this point, coaches can feel an overwhelming temptation to tell teachers what they should do, solving their problems for them. Doing this, however, keeps the collaborating teacher from solving and owning the problem, creates dependency, demotivates the teacher, and often results in a weak solution to the wrong problem (Stanier, 2020).

But what if the teacher *really* doesn't know what to do? What if the teacher is struggling with classroom management and the coach is a highly proficient trainer on that very topic? Should the coach just keep all that information in like a poker player trying to hide a royal flush? The answer is yes and no. The coach should not tell the teacher what do to. However, when—and only when—it is truly needed, the coach should share ideas in a tentative way, while ensuring that the teacher is the eventual decision maker. The coach, in other words, should share ideas dialogically, balancing telling with asking.

I usually start this conversation by asking teachers to suggest some strategies they think might help them meet their goals. I find it important to write down these suggestions, as the simple act of creating a list encourages both the teacher and me to add more possibilities to the list ("Let's see if we can come up with one or two more strategies"); demonstrates that I have heard and value my collaborating teacher's ideas; and ensures that I don't forget any suggestions.

I usually suggest to the teacher that we try to come up with four to six teaching strategies. If the teacher seems stuck, I ask questions to prompt deeper reflection, like "What advice would you give someone trying to hit this goal?" or "How have you addressed this issue with other students or while teaching other content?" If the teacher's words or body language suggest that she is really stuck and needs some suggestions, I ask, "Would you mind if I share a few thoughts about how you might reach your goal?"

When the teacher does want suggestions, I explain my ideas and ask if I should add them to our list. At this point in the conversation, I have to guard against overvaluing my suggestions. The moment I appear to be pushing for a particular strategy, I extinguish the opportunity for dialogue.

Sometimes the teacher suggests a strategy that I think could fail—say, using cooperative learning in a class where many student are off task. At that point, I might again ask for permission to share my ideas, and if the teacher grants me permission, I might say, "Now, you know your students better than I do, so you'll know what's best here, but I've found that if you don't have clear expectations for behavior in place before using cooperative learning, students often get more off task. What do you think about that?"

Once we've got a list, I read back every suggestion in the order I noted them and ask a question like "Which of these options gives you the most confidence?" or "Which of these options brings you the most energy?" All options, regardless of whose idea they are, must be given equal consideration so the teacher feels free to pick the one that makes the most sense to her.

For this conversation to work, the coach must work from the Partnership Principles and bear in mind the conditions for dialogue identified by Paulo Freire (1970). That is, the coach must be humble—to me, humility is the only appropriate response to the complexities of the classroom. The coach must show faith in the teacher, by encouraging her to share ideas and making sure she makes the decisions about what happens in the classroom. Finally, the coach must obviously have the teacher's best interest at heart. A conversation about strategies that is truly a dialogue empowers and energizes both the teacher and the coach.

Questions to Identify a Strategy
- What teaching strategy could you use to meet this goal?
- What advice would you give someone who is trying to meet this goal?
- How have you successfully addressed this issue with other students or while teaching other content?
- Do you mind if I share a few thoughts about what you might do to meet this goal?
- Which of these options gives you the most confidence?
- Which of these options brings you the most energy?

Note: These are based on questions I have learned from John Campbell and Christian van Nieuwerburgh.

Stage Two: Learn

After the collaborating teacher has identified (1) a clear picture of reality, (2) a goal based on that picture of reality, and (3) a strategy for meeting the goal, the coach should ensure that the teacher is ready to use the strategy. Usually, the coach describes or co-constructs a description of the strategy and ensures that the teacher sees it being used by one or more educators.

Step 1: Explain strategies

One of the first things I discovered as I studied professional development was that checklists greatly improve the clarity and power of explanations. They help coaches lay out the steps of a teaching strategy, keep coaches from skipping important elements of a strategy during an explanation, and compel coaches to get a deep understanding of the practices they share. The best checklists are simple but comprehensive, making it easy for teachers to implement the strategies.

Again, coaches need to resist the temptation to give advice when they explain strategies. They must balance telling with asking, using the checklist to explain strategies directly and clearly and also asking teachers throughout the explanation to share any changes they would like to make that would better meet the needs of students.

When coaches balance telling with asking, they say what they think while making it easy for teachers to say what *they* think, too. Done well, such dialogical conversations are collaborative, open, free, and energizing exchanges where everyone honestly says what they think.

There are some simple things a coach can do to balance telling with asking. For example, at the start of an explanation, she should explain that she has two major goals: (1) to go through the checklist so the teacher clearly understands the strategy, and (2) to record any changes the teacher wants to make to the strategy. Next, the coach should provide a quick description of the strategy and give the teacher a chance to read the checklist. Before exploring the strategy more deeply, the coach should ask the teacher to share any preliminary questions or comments about the checklist.

Once the teacher has looked over the checklist, the coach should go through it item by item and ask the teacher if the explanation is clear and whether the teacher would like to modify any of the items. The coach should write down on the checklist any modifications the teacher would like to make. If the teacher suggests modifications that the coach believes will make the strategy significantly less effective, the coach should share her thoughts with the teacher while still positioning the teacher as the decision maker in the conversation.

After they have discussed all the items on the checklist, the coach should sum up how it appears the teacher will use the strategy and ask if anything is still unclear. Then, the coach should ask, "Now that we've gone through this, on a scale of 1 to 10, how confident are you that you can implement this practice?" If the teacher doesn't feel confident, the coach and teacher should go back through the checklist until the teacher is ready to use the strategy in the classroom.

During a dialogical explanation, the coach must listen to the teacher's comments without judgment, share (in a dialogical way) any thoughts about the checklist she may have, explore with the teacher where those thoughts lead, and modify the checklist with any teacher-led suggestions.

Some researchers and professional developers are challenged by the idea behind dialogical explanations, asking, "Doesn't the teacher have to teach the strategy with fidelity?" But fidelity of implementation is not the actual goal here. The purpose of instructional coaching is to unmistakably improve students' learning and well-being, as summarized in the PEERS goal identified by the teacher. The PEERS goal is an objective standard for excellence, ensuring that the teacher implements teaching strategies effectively. This often means that a strategy is implemented with fidelity, but not always. Sometimes a strategy has to be adapted for particular students or teachers to work. Other times, too strict a focus on fidelity can keep a teacher from meeting the goal. If a goal isn't met, the teacher will have many opportunities during the Improve stage of the cycle to identify what to change and, in partnership with the coach, how to adapt the strategy for success.

One of the strengths of a dialogical approach to explanations is that it makes the teacher's thinking visible. When teachers feel comfortable telling coaches how they might change a strategy, coaches have a chance to discuss the implications of doing so. But if a coach simply tells a teacher how a strategy must be taught, any opportunity for a reflective conversation is lost and the teacher is silenced. Ironically, telling a teacher how a strategy must be taught can sometimes decrease fidelity to a practice.

Step 2: Model strategies

It is helpful for teachers to see a strategy being used in the classroom before implementing it themselves. In many cases, the easiest way for this to happen is for the coach to model the strategy in the teacher's classroom. The coach should apply the strategy competently but realistically, without over-shadowing the teacher, and talk positively about the teacher to the students during the lesson. The teacher can follow along during modeling by consulting a checklist that the coach provides. Teachers have told us they usually don't want the coach to teach the entire lesson—they just want to see the strategy they are learning.

Modeling in the teacher's classroom isn't always the best approach, however. A coach who takes control of a class where behavior management is the issue, for example, can unintentionally erode the teacher's already shaky powerbase. Also, if the coach isn't able to control the class, not much will be learned. Modeling in a teacher's classroom also may not be the best idea if a coach doesn't know the content being taught. In that situation, it might be better for the coach to co-teach with the teacher. The coach can demonstrate the strategy while the teacher covers the content.

Coaches can also model strategies for teachers without students in the room. One obvious disadvantage of this method is that it is artificial; both the teacher and the coach have to imagine what it would look like if students *were* in the class. On the plus side, the teacher can stop the coach at any point during the demonstration and ask questions or ask the coach to repeat an action to make it clearer.

Another option is for teachers to go to other teachers' classrooms and watch their peers use a strategy. The coach and teacher can go together to observe the class, or the coach can teach the collaborating teacher's class while the teacher conducts the observation. Teachers will find it helpful to bring a checklist to the class to focus their observations. After watching the lesson, if time permits, the coach, the modeling teacher, and the collaborating teacher can get together to discuss the lesson.

Sometimes, coaches partner with teachers to set up model classrooms where teachers teach many or all of the teaching strategies in the coach's playbook. This approach requires the coach to spend a lot of time describing and modeling lessons for the classroom teacher and the classroom teacher to spend a lot time learning the new strategies, but it can be very helpful.

Many coaches around the world are building libraries of videos that show teachers implementing teaching strategies. Coaches report that teachers find these videos helpful. (Of course, the recordings are only taken with the teachers' permission.)

Finally, coaches may offer teachers a combination of ways to see a model of a lesson. For example, they might show a video of a teacher using a strategy and then co-teach with the teacher until the teacher feels ready to implement the strategy independently. There are many different combinations to try out. What matters is that afterward the collaborating teacher feels confident about applying the new strategy. And that's when the real fun starts.

Stage Three: Improve

In a perfect world, a teacher who has learned a new strategy would implement it and students would immediately meet their achievement or engagement goals. Unfortunately, our world is less than perfect. Most of the time, the teacher has to modify or replace the initial strategy or goal so that it works with students. This, in a nutshell, is the collaborative work of the Improve stage: making adaptations until a goal is met. This stage involves four steps.

Step 1: Confirm direction

Every time the coach and teacher meet, the coach should start by checking to see if the collaborating teacher has anything to discuss before starting the formal coaching conversation. Sometimes teachers are so focused on a certain issue, such as a student success or a disappointing evaluation, that they aren't ready to talk about, say, data or instructional practices. If the topic at the front of the teacher's mind is ignored, the conversation won't be successful. Confirming questions like the two in the following box can help ensure that the coaching conversation focuses on the teacher's main concerns.

Questions to Confirm Direction
- What's on your mind? (Michael Bungay Stanier)
- Given the time we have today, what is the most important thing for us to talk about? (Susan Scott)

Step 2: Review progress

When the teacher is ready, the coach should ask to discuss whatever progress students have made toward the goal and what the teacher is learning about the strategy, the students, or himself. When coaches partner with teachers to review progress, they often find the following questions to be helpful.

Questions to Review Progress
- What has gone well?
- What are you seeing that shows this strategy is successful?
- What progress has been made toward the goal?
- What did you learn?
- What surprised you? (Barkley, 2009)
- What roadblocks are you running into?

Step 3: Invent improvements

When reviewing progress, the teacher and coach will inevitably transition to exploring what changes need to be made to ensure success. The teacher can only make a limited number of changes to ensure improvements: to the way the strategy is taught, to the strategy itself, to the goal, or to the kind of data gathered to show progress toward the goal.

During the Improve stage, coaches often use the following Improve questions.

Questions to Improve Practice
- Do you want to keep using the strategy as it is?
- Do you want to revisit how you use the teaching strategy?
- Do you want to choose a new strategy?
- Do you want to change the way you measure progress toward the goal?
- Do you want to change the goal?

Step 4: Plan next steps

Before ending the conversation, the coach should make sure that the teacher has developed a clear plan for next steps. To do so, the coach should ask the teacher what tasks need to be completed in the next week, when each task will be completed, and who will do it (usually the teacher). The coach should carefully note down the details of the plan and email the notes to the collaborating teacher right after the conversation.

Before ending the session, I like to ask one last question: "On a scale of 1 to 10, how committed are you to this goal now?" If the collaborating teacher gives me a high number, we bring the session to a close. If the number is low, I continue the conversation by asking a question like "What needs to change to move you closer to a 10?"

Coaches and teachers should meet at least once a week. Meeting too frequently can interfere with reflection; teachers need time to think for themselves, and that's hard to do if they're meeting every day with the coach. At the same time, if the coach and teacher don't meet at least once a week, the collaboration might lose its sense of urgency. Ultimately, the coach and teacher need to meet frequently enough to make steady progress toward the goal.

Questions to Plan for Next Steps
- When should we meet again?
- What tasks have to be done before we meet?

- When will those tasks be done?
- Who will do them?
- On a scale of 1 to 10, how committed are you to this goal now?

To Sum Up

The Impact Cycle involves three stages: Identify, Learn, and Improve.

Identify. During this stage, coaches partner with teachers so teachers can identify a clear picture of reality (such as by reviewing a video of a lesson, learning from student interviews, reviewing student work, or analyzing observation data gathered by the coach). After this, coaches partner with teachers so that teachers can set a goal that is powerful, easy, emotionally compelling, reachable, and student-focused (i.e., a PEERS goal). Next, coaches partner with teachers to identify a strategy that teachers will implement in an attempt to meet the goal.

Learn. During this stage, coaches partner with teachers to ensure that they are ready to implement the strategy they have chosen. Often this involves clear but dialogical explanations of a teaching strategy (frequently involving a checklist) and modeling, which could involve coaches modeling in collaborating teachers' classrooms (with or without students present), coaches co-teaching, teachers visiting colleagues' classrooms, teachers watching a video of the strategy being taught, or several of these learning opportunities in combination.

Improve. During this stage, coaches and teachers collaborate to make adaptations until goals are met. These collaborations may involve changing how strategies are taught, changing strategies, changing goals, changing the kinds of data gathered to show progress toward goals, or simply waiting for the change to work.

Reflection Questions

1. What happens during coaching when teachers do not have a clear picture of reality in their classroom?

2. What difference does it make when teachers are (or are not) emotionally committed to meeting the goals they set?

3. Do you have a collection of teaching strategies that you can share with teachers to help them meet their goals?

4. Have you used checklists? If so, did they help? If not, would you consider using them?

5. How important is it to see a strategy before you teach it?

6. What do you do to ensure that teachers go all the way through the cycle and meet their goals?

Going Deeper

The Impact Cycle presented here is more extensively described in my book *The Impact Cycle* (Knight, 2018). That book provides an in-depth discussion of the cycle and includes many tools. But it should be read with this chapter in mind, because here I describe many refinements that have been made to the cycle since that book was published, including those related to the pre-cycle conversations, identifying strategies, and explaining strategies. The Impact Cycle was influenced by the following books that would also be helpful to anyone who is interested in being a change leader.

- Atul Gawande's book *The Checklist Manifesto* (2011) is a helpful and beautifully written book for anyone who has to explain things to other people, which is pretty much all of us. Gawande's TED Talk (2017) on coaching is also a must-watch for anyone even slightly interested in coaching.

- Chip and Dan Heath's *Switch* (2010) and Heidi Grant-Halvorson's *Nine Things Successful People Do Differently* (2012) taught me a lot about leading change and setting goals. (A cool feature of Grant-Halvorson's book, if you read it on the Kindle, is that the Kindle text includes links to the research articles that the author mentions to support her assertions.)

- Grant-Halvorson's *No One Understands You and What to Do About It* (2015) offers a great summary of the perceptual errors described here.

- Two books that have greatly improved my ability to ask questions (and to be a better coach in general) are John Campbell and Christian van

Nieuwerburgh's *The Leader's Guide to Coaching in Schools* (2018) and van Nieuwerburgh's *An Introduction to Coaching Skills* (2017), which I consider an essential text for coaches.

What's Next?

Trying to learn how to coach well without implementing an Impact Cycle is like trying to learn how to swim without ever getting into the water—totally counterproductive. Because completing a cycle can be intimidating, I suggest coaches consider the first few cycles they engage in primarily as opportunities to learn, perhaps starting out with a friendly colleague who will offer plenty of support. Once coaches are moving through the cycle, they should address all seven of the Success Factors identified in this book.

A coach will likely need a playbook and will need to know how to gather data and how to listen and ask questions effectively before succeeding in the role, but real learning starts with the coaching cycle, and coaches need to start moving through it as soon as possible. If they plan to call themselves coaches, coaches need to start coaching.

Learning Map for Chapter 5

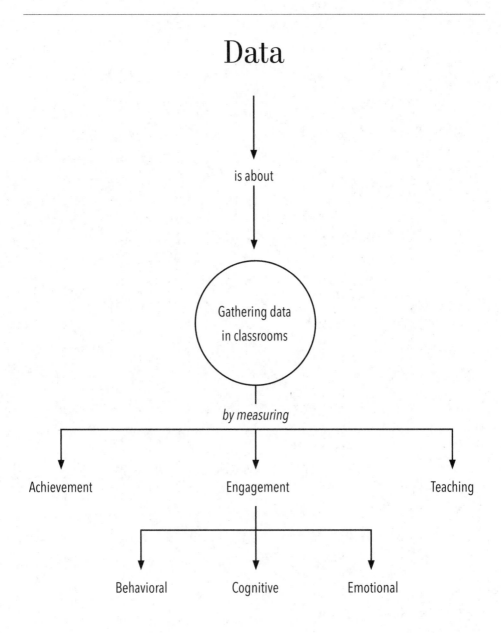

Data

is about

Gathering data
in classrooms

by measuring

Achievement   Engagement   Teaching

Behavioral   Cognitive   Emotional

5 Data

All data are wrong, but some are useful.

—With apologies to statistician George Box

Mark Dowley is the director of staff development and instruction at Brighton Grammar School, a prestigious independent boys' school in Melbourne, Australia. When Mark and Brighton Grammar's deputy headmaster, Ray Swann, came to ICG's Intensive Instructional Coaching Institute, one of the most significant ideas they took away was the importance of gathering data during coaching.

"Brighton Grammar has been teaching students from 3-year-olds to 18-year-olds for decades," Mark told me. In recent years, Ray, Mark, and their colleagues have turned Brighton Grammar into a pioneering school promoting evidence-based practice. They have partnered with John Hattie and his colleagues to promote Visible Learning, and the school has placed a heavy emphasis on student well-being. "At the core of everything," Mark said, "is the Impact Cycle: Identify, Learn, Improve."

Data are central to coaching at Brighton Grammar. Mark told me about his coaching partnership with one teacher, whom I'll call Jane Sheridan. Jane's class was in trouble. According to Mark, "Students weren't learning; they weren't engaged. They were often disrespectful to each other and to the teacher. It was the kind of class where, when you walk past the classroom and look in, you say, 'Now that's not how school should be.'"

Jane felt overwhelmed and stressed because the deputy headmaster was getting complaints from parents. "As a teacher, this can keep you awake at night," Mark said.

Mark offered to observe Jane's class and gather data. He found that time on task—one way of measuring whether students appear to be engaged in class—was at a dismal 30 percent. To improve those numbers, Jane and Mark started by focusing on the first 10 minutes of class, introducing some teaching routines to get things started smoothly. Jane worked really hard, and soon, time on task increased to around 80 percent for those first 10 minutes. These data showed Jane that the issue wasn't the boys just being disruptive and uninterested. "She could see that the boys really could engage," said Mark, "and that built her motivation to carry on for the rest of the class." After more hard work, Jane eventually was able to get overall time on task up to 70 percent. She started to enjoy the class and built much stronger relationships with the students. "Data helped me track growth," Mark said, "and that's probably one of the most powerful things you can do because the teachers' attitude to the class, their students, and their job improves dramatically."

Data are also central to the continuous improvement of the school. Mark explained that the school uses the Kirkpatrick model (Kirkpatrick Partners, 2009) for evaluating professional development by asking, "Was it relevant?" "Did I learn something new?" "Did I apply what I learned?" and "Did it have an impact on students?" The data from that evaluation have helped them evaluate and justify the use of the Impact Cycle. Compared with the impact of whole-staff presentations and external professional learning activities, results for the Impact Cycle "were through the roof," according to Mark.

Word is spreading in Melbourne about Brighton Grammar School's partnership approach to coaching. In fact, as Mark explained to me, the school's coaching model is attracting excellent teachers. "People see what we're doing in coaching," he said, "and they want to be part of a community that trusts their staff, values their staff, and partners with their staff."

When I contacted Mark to fact-check this story, he had more good news. Brighton Grammar's median Australian Tertiary Admission Rank (ATAR) score was the highest ever—87.95. The school's overall rank in the Australian state of Victoria had moved up from 65th to 19th, and it had shown its best scores since coaching was implemented. Additionally, staff well-being scores on an assessment of support, kindness, perseverance, pride in work, and enthusiasm were all between 89 and 93 percent. "Despite the [COVID-19] lockdown and distance/remote learning, our school achieved its best-ever results this year," Mark wrote me. "I'd like to think a large part of that is due to us focusing on the Partnership Principles and coaching."

Why Coaches Need to Gather Data

We see the value of data everywhere, every day. On a winter morning, we check our weather app to see the temperature and windchill factor so we can know how to dress. If we go for an early-morning run, we use an app to track how fast and how far we run. If we are trying get in shape, we might get on the scale to see our weight and then type the number of calories from our breakfast into a weight-loss app. And all this happens before we even really start the day!

Data are just as central to instructional coaches' work. They help both teachers and coaches see more of what is happening in the classroom, help teachers establish goals and measure progress toward goals, and build teacher efficacy by demonstrating the progress that is being made.

Data Help Us See More

When I studied English literature in graduate school, I came to see how specific kinds of knowledge could help me see more in the poetry and prose that I read. When I read Walter Jackson Bate's (1963) biography of John Keats, for example, I learned that Keats lived by the sea while writing "The Fall of Hyperion." That knowledge gave me a whole new insight into the rhythm, meter, and structure of Keats's incomplete epic poem.

You may have had a similar experience when you learned a new word and then heard that word used in the following days, or when you bought a new car and felt like suddenly you saw that model everywhere. Obviously, your new car hasn't suddenly become wildly popular; what has changed is that a piece of knowledge has shaped your perception so that you see more than you did previously.

I refer to this experience as using an *interpretive lens*. Looking at Keats's poem through the interpretive lens of the sea, I gained a deeper understanding of the poem's rhythm. During instructional coaching, data make for a similarly powerful interpretive lens. Used effectively, they reveal aspects of a learning experience that we would not otherwise see. For example, data about time spent on task helped Jane Sheridan at Brighton Grammar School to better understand how many students were and were not involved in the learning. Similarly, data from formative assessment help teachers better understand how students are learning. Put simply, data make the invisible visible.

Data Help Establish Goals

Data also bring precision to goal setting by providing a clear finish line. If I say that I want to run a 5K in less than 21 minutes (I wish!) or that I want at least 90 percent of my students to be able to write a well-organized paragraph as assessed by a single-point rubric, it's the precision that makes these goals actionable. When I have a clear view of my destination, I am much more likely to get there.

Data Help Measure Progress

Data also help us measure progress. A runner who is training to set a personal record will likely time her runs to see if she is getting faster. Similarly, a teacher who wants to improve student learning or well-being can gather data to see if the changes he is making are having an impact.

Data also show teachers whether what they are doing is working. Often, the first changes teachers make do not lead directly to students hitting the PEERS goals discussed in Chapter 4. Adaptations almost always have to be made, and data reveal which changes are working.

Data Help Build Teacher Efficacy

Finally, data also build efficacy. As Mark Dowley found at Brighton Grammar School, when data show that students are more successful or more engaged, teachers and coaches see that their efforts are making a difference. Theresa Amabile and Steven Kramer (2011) label this the "progress principle." They write:

> Facilitating progress is the most effective way for managers to influence inner work life. Even when progress happens in small steps, a person's sense of steady forward movement toward an important goal can make all the difference between a great day and a terrible one. (pp. 76–77)

Six Data Rules

Teachers and coaches need data to establish goals, monitor progress, make adaptations, and increase efficacy. However, data are only helpful when used well. I have identified six rules that will help you use data more effectively.

Data Should Be Chosen by the Teacher

Teachers will be most motivated, and consequently will learn the most, when they choose the data that are gathered during coaching. This doesn't mean a coach can't suggest types of data to gather. In fact, in some cases, teachers won't know what data could be gathered and, therefore, will want and need suggestions from their coach. Effective coaches master the art of suggesting types of data while still positioning the teacher as the decision maker in the conversation.

Data Should Be Objective

You can see the difference between objective and subjective data if you watch the Winter Olympics. During speed skating, where the data are objective, whoever makes it to the finish line in the shortest amount of time goes home with the gold medal. Because the data are objective, assuming everyone is judged to have raced fairly, there are very few controversies about who wins. This is how objective data work. There is very little opinion involved; data just are what they are.

But during figure skating, where the data are subjective, the experience is often quite different. Figure skaters, or at least figure skating commentators, often criticize the subjective way in which skaters are scored. Since subjective data, by definition, involve the observer's opinion, conversations about them can turn away from what happened and toward whether or not a given opinion is accurate.

Objective data are not personal—they're factual. When coaches gather and share reliable, objective data, their opinion shouldn't guide the conversation; they are just reporting the facts. Objective data keep the focus where it should be—on students and teaching.

Data Should Be Gathered Frequently

A GPS that only tells us when we have arrived at our destination wouldn't be of much help. The same is true for data gathered in the classroom. Data won't help teachers and coaches monitor progress if they are only collected once or twice a year. Instead, data need to be gathered at least weekly. Teachers and coaches need the feedback provided by frequently gathered data because teachers usually need to adjust how strategies are used until those strategies help students move closer to their goals. Data only help us see what is working and what needs to change when they are gathered frequently.

Data Should Be Valid

Valid data measure what they are intended to measure. For example, a valid measurement of whether someone can ride a bicycle would be the act of either riding or failing to ride one; asking the person to complete a multiple-choice test on bicycle riding would be less valid. So, too, in the classroom: teachers and coaches need to make sure that the data they gather actually measure what students are supposed to be learning.

Data Should Be Reliable and Mutually Understood

When several coaches gather the same type of data and get the same results, we say that their results are reliable. As a general rule, researchers strive for a reliability score of higher than 95 percent.

In coaching, reliability can have a slightly different meaning. During coaching, it is most important that the coach and teacher agree on (1) what data to gather, (2) how the data are gathered, and (3) why the data are gathered. There should be no surprises when it comes to data gathering.

One way to increase mutual understanding is for the coach and teacher to create a T-chart that depicts examples and nonexamples of whatever data are being gathered, such as the one shown in Figure 5.1.

Data Should Be Gathered by Teachers When Possible

Coaches have told us that when teachers gather and analyze their own data, they are much more likely to accept the data and change their behavior as needed. The easiest way for teachers to do this is by video-recording their lessons, which also lets observers watch segments of a lesson multiple times to clarify what happened. When the observer is also the teacher, such data can especially lead to powerful learning.

The six data rules should inform how coaches and teachers gather data of all types. What those types actually are constitutes much of the rest of this chapter.

Engagement Data

Students who stay in school do so because they feel they belong, they have hope, they feel safe, and they feel engaged by school. In fact, engagement is the main reason students who stay in school do so (Knight, 2019). If we want students to experience happiness, have healthy relationships, be productive, and graduate, we must do what we can to ensure they are engaged. To do this, we need to first know what we mean by engagement. For that reason, I have broken this discussion down into three categories: *behavioral, cognitive,* and *emotional engagement.*

FIGURE 5.1

Time-on-Task T-Chart

Time on Task Is . . .	Time on Task Is Not . . .
Listening to direct instruction	Engaging in side conversations
Using technology for learning	Playing with technology
Participating in . . .	Bothering other students
classroom discussion	Sleeping
group work	Being out of seat without permission
partner talk	Failing to take out materials
Doing activities such as practice, test taking, and so on	Doing other activities such as reading or homework for another class
Taking notes	Texting

Behavioral Engagement

To better understand the different types of data, let's imagine an instructional coach—we'll call her Tamika Rohl—who works in a middle school in a midwestern U.S. city. Tamika is a qualified and effective coach who is well liked and respected by her colleagues. Listening in on Tamika's typical coaching conversations will help us understand the different ways coaches can gather data.

One of the teachers Tamika is partnering with is Allie Sherman, a third-year 7th grade science teacher. Allie loves science, and her enthusiasm goes a long way toward keeping students with her, but she wants to be better. She asks Tamika to partner with her, and they kick off the Impact Cycle with Tamika video-recording a lesson.

Allie and Tamika review the video separately. They both see that, while Allie's students enjoy being in class, they present some challenging behaviors. Students blurted out joking comments during instruction, and many of them engaged in side conversations while Allie was teaching. At different times, Allie politely corrected students, but the students only changed their behavior temporarily. On four different occasions, she asked two students to stop talking, but at the end of the lesson, the same two students were still conversing.

Measuring behavioral engagement

After watching Allie's class, Tamika wonders if Allie will want to set a behavioral goal. Tamika frequently uses four different measures she could share with Allie to assess behavioral engagement: (1) time on task, (2) disruptions, (3) student responses, and (4) incivility.

Time on task. Time on task assesses whether students are doing what the teacher wants them to do. It is one of the most frequently gathered measures, but it has its limitations. On the one hand, it is easy to gather reliable data on time spent on task; on the other hand, time on task tells us only whether students *appear* to be doing what they're supposed to be doing. They could be totally immersed in their learning experiences—or they could be confused, or thinking about something unrelated to learning. However, in a class like Allie's, where many students are off task, increasing the number of students who are on task can be a powerful first step forward.

Disruptions. A second measure of behavioral engagement is disruptions —the number of times students say or do things that interrupt the teacher's teaching or other students' learning. In a classroom with too many disruptions, students struggle to learn, teachers struggle to teach, and everyone struggles to remain positive and energized. For these reasons, Allie might want to choose reducing disruptions as her goal.

Student responses. In engaged classrooms, most, if not all, students are involved in discussions. Allie might choose to measure how often and how many different students respond to questions.

Incivility. Students find it difficult to learn when they are afraid that they will be insulted, put down, attacked with a sarcastic remark, or made to feel "stupid" or inadequate. There is no room for bullying and verbal abuse in any classroom, anywhere. Tamika or Allie could gather data on incivility to gauge the mood and psychological safety of Allie's classroom—an important action for any educator.

How to gather behavioral data

When Tamika meets with Allie, she doesn't come in with a plan for her. Instead, she asks Allie to describe what she notices on the video. If Allie isn't sure what her goal should be, Tamika is ready to share some options, but Allie knows what she wants to improve. She feels that if students are engaged, they'll probably be less disruptive, so she sets a goal that at least 90 percent of her students will consistently be on task.

Tamika finds that the easiest and most helpful way to gather behavioral data is to record it on the seating chart for the class being observed. In Allie's class, she uses the existing seating chart. In classes where teachers don't use a seating chart, she quickly sketches one for the purpose of gathering data. When students are not sitting at desks, she tallies them.

Tamika gathers time-on-task data by looking at each student, noting whether they are on task, and marking it on the seating chart by using a plus mark for on-task behavior and a minus mark for off-task behavior (see Figure 5.2). Tamika usually records data every 5 or 10 minutes, but always makes sure to ask teachers when they would like data to be gathered. (Some teachers want the data to be gathered in the middle of each activity, for example.)

Tamika also records other types of data on seating charts, such as disruptions, responses, or incivility. Disruptions and responses are fairly easy to identify and tally, but incivility requires a little more discussion. To measure it, coaches and teachers need to determine what they consider to be an uncivil interaction. Typically, insults, hateful statements, put-downs, and sarcastic comments are considered uncivil. Additionally, the teacher and coach might identify forms of uncivil nonverbal communication.

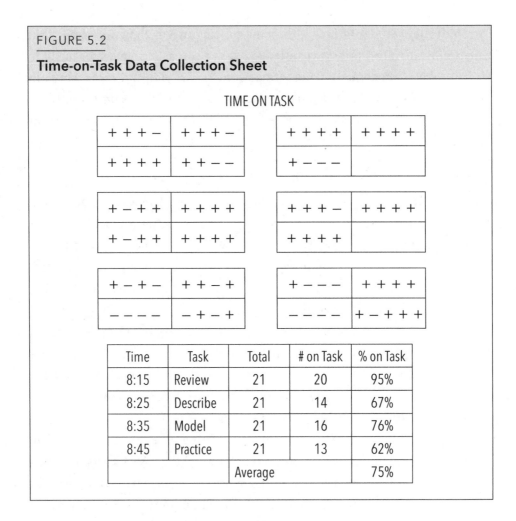

FIGURE 5.2

Time-on-Task Data Collection Sheet

TIME ON TASK

Time	Task	Total	# on Task	% on Task
8:15	Review	21	20	95%
8:25	Describe	21	14	67%
8:35	Model	21	16	76%
8:45	Practice	21	13	62%
		Average		75%

Cognitive Engagement

Tamika also partners with Jacob Robinson, who has been teaching mathematics in the school for about 10 years. To get started, Jacob agrees to watch a video recording of one of his lessons. When Jacob and Tamika first meet, after separately watching the video, Jacob says that he is most concerned that his students didn't seem to see the value of what they were learning in his class. "These kids are hearing about stuff that will be really important for them as they move up through high school and hopefully to college," he says, "but they won't learn it if they aren't engaged." "What I wonder," Tamika suggests, "is what kind of engagement most concerns you." Then, after asking

Jacob for his permission, she explains the differences between behavioral, cognitive, and emotional engagement.

Tamika and Jacob quickly agree that behavioral engagement isn't an issue in his class, so Tamika goes on to explain cognitive engagement. When students are cognitively engaged, they experience what their teacher intends for them to experience during an activity. Cognitive engagement is similar to what Phil Schlechty (2011) calls "authentic engagement," which he contrasts with "strategic compliance." According to Schlechty, students who are strategically compliant do activities for strategic reasons—to earn praise, for example, or to get a better grade—rather than because they see the activities as meaningful, relevant, or enjoyable.

By contrast, students who are cognitively engaged (or as Schlechty would say, authentically engaged) find meaning and value in learning tasks. They are attentive, committed, and persistent until they complete tasks because they see the value in them. When students are cognitively engaged, they are more motivated, more positive, and most likely learning more than students who are not engaged.

Measuring cognitive engagement

Tamika explains to Jacob that they can assess cognitive engagement in different ways. And since cognitive engagement occurs *within* students, the best strategy is to ask students to describe how engaged they are.

Interviewing students. One option for gathering data is for Tamika to ask Jacob's students about their perceptions of the class. Alternatively, she could teach Jacob's class to free him up to interview students; however, students might be more forthcoming with a coach than with their teacher.

When coaches sit down and talk with students, they can learn a lot about how students are experiencing a particular class or even school in general. For interviews, teachers should identify a small sample of students in a class—perhaps one-fifth—choosing a cross section of students who will share the most useful information. The wider the range of students interviewed, the more useful the data will be.

The following are some sample questions for assessing cognitive engagement, but teachers and coaches should think carefully about what they want to learn from students and draft their own.

Sample Cognitive Engagement Questions

Note: Questions should be modified for content and students' ages.

- What's the best thing about this class?
- What's the worst thing about this class?
- What could make this class a better learning experience for you?
- How do you feel when you walk into this classroom?
- What do other students say about this class?
- How would you describe this class?
- How confident are you that you will do great in this class? What could increase your confidence that you will succeed?
- Does this class really matter to you? If so, why? If not, what would have to change to make this class matter to you?

Exit tickets. Coaches and teachers get a lot of useful information when they interview students, but interviews are hard to schedule more than once or twice a semester. Besides, they sample only a fraction of the students in a classroom. Another way for teachers to better understand their students' cognitive engagement is to ask students to complete exit tickets once a week.

An exit ticket is a slip of paper or an index card with one or more questions on it. Some exit tickets include a scale question for students to answer ("On a scale of 1 to 6, how meaningful was the work in class last week?"). For younger students, they could feature emojis rather than numbers on a scale. Exit tickets can also be designed to ask students what their teacher can do to help them be more engaged ("What can I do to make this class more meaningful to you?"). Students complete exit tickets at the end of the period and turn them in to their teacher as they leave the classroom.

Exit tickets are powerful, but they aren't always valid; many students overestimate their level of engagement. Often, the most important piece of data on an exit ticket is what students say about how the class could be changed to be more engaging.

Correct academic responses. Another way to assess cognitive engagement is to identify the percentage of students who give correct answers to the teacher's questions, often referred to as correct academic responses (CAR). Tamika could gather this type of data in Jacob's class using a seating chart. Like other kinds of data, CAR data are helpful but imperfect. Learning involves risks, and wrong answers can be better indications of learning than correct ones. Additionally, a 100 percent CAR rate for an entire class, while appearing to be a positive, may suggest that the content is not sufficiently challenging. Teachers and coaches may find it helpful to gather this type of data along with the number of different students responding. If the CAR rate is 93 percent but only 18 percent of students responded to questions, we cannot assume all students understand the content.

Experience sampling. The idea behind this powerful method is simple: Each student has a copy of a form like the one shown in Figure 5.3, and the teacher or coach sets up a timer to go off every 10 minutes during a lesson. Each time the timer goes off, students rank their current level of engagement on the form, with 1 indicating they are not engaged at all and 6 indicating they are completely engaged. Students can also write about what the teacher could do to make learning more engaging.

Teachers may find it helpful to audio- or video-record their lesson and then replay the recording as they review the forms the students have completed. Teachers can slide the recording to the points where the timer went off (usually every 10 minutes) to see what was happening when students completed their form, gaining insight into their responses.

One other obvious and powerful way to measure cognitive engagement is to assess whether students have learned the content, which I discuss later in this chapter.

Emotional Engagement

Jacob isn't sure that cognitive engagement is the most important goal for his students. "What I really want is for my students to feel totally safe speaking out and asking questions," he says. "I want them to be totally OK with sharing whatever is going on in their heads." Hearing this, and with Jacob's permission, Tamika describes another type of data: emotional engagement. She explains that students who are emotionally engaged see their experiences in school as positive and meaningful, feel they belong in their school, feel physically and psychologically safe, have friends, and have hope. In short, emotional engagement measures connectedness, belonging, and physical and psychological safety.

FIGURE 5.3					
Experience Sampling Form: Cognitive Engagement					
Engaged?					
Each time you hear the bell, please rate your level of engagement in the learning.					
No					Yes
1	2	3	4	5	6
1	2	3	4	5	6
1	2	3	4	5	6
1	2	3	4	5	6
1	2	3	4	5	6
1	2	3	4	5	6
1	2	3	4	5	6
1	2	3	4	5	6
1	2	3	4	5	6
1	2	3	4	5	6

Measuring emotional engagement

Tamika tells Jacob that she can assess emotional engagement using many of the measures she would use for cognitive engagement. Again, the best data often come from the students themselves.

Interviewing students. Tamika notes that, as with cognitive engagement, she can interview students to understand their level of emotional engagement. Since emotional engagement can have many dimensions—safety, relationships, hope, well-being—Jacob would have to carefully consider what questions would be most important to ask before they conducted interviews. Fortunately, many resources are available that Jacob and Tamika can review to help them create the questions that would be most helpful in their situation.

For example, the Gallup Student Poll (Gallup, 2020) includes the following five statements that may be adapted and used as questions for interviews related to emotional engagement:

- I have a best friend at school.
- I feel safe in this school.
- My teachers make me feel my schoolwork is important.
- I have the opportunity to do what I do best every day.
- In the last seven days, I have received recognition or praise for schoolwork.

Another option is to use questions stemming from Martin Seligman's acronym PERMA, which stands for positive emotion, engagement, relationships, meaning, and accomplishment (2011, pp. 16–17).

- **Positive Emotion:** How happy and satisfied were you last week?
- **Engagement:** How often were you completely engaged in learning activities in this class last week?
- **Relationships:** How positive were your interactions with other people last week?
- **Meaning:** How meaningful were your experiences last week?
- **Accomplishment:** How proud are you of what you accomplished last week?

Finally, research on hope (Lopez, 2013)—which identifies goals, pathways, and agency as essential components—provides another way to ask students about their engagement.

- **Goal:** What is your goal for next week in this class?
- **Pathways:** What are you going to do to hit your goal?
- **Agency:** How confident are you that you will hit your goal?

Exit tickets. Exit tickets are my favorite way of assessing emotional engagement. Students can complete an exit ticket on the same topic each week. The assessments could be about hope, meaning, positive experiences, happiness, relationships, or some other topic. If teachers include a scale, they can get a quick read on students' level of emotional engagement ("On a scale of 1 to 6, how safe do you feel speaking up in class?") while also gathering insight about what they themselves can do to help ("What could I do to make this class an even safer place for you?"). Again, exit tickets for younger students could feature emojis rather than numbers.

Other methods for assessing emotional engagement. Emotional engagement can also be assessed through the use of interactive journals in which students and teachers write back and forth to each other each week. Journals build connections with students, which is important, but students may be less candid in their journals than on anonymous exit tickets.

Many of the educators we meet tell us that they see emotional engagement as a prerequisite for all learning. Students who feel alone, afraid, or hopeless will struggle to learn until those factors are addressed. This is why coaching that focuses entirely on achievement runs the risk of not addressing students' greatest needs.

Let me be clear, though: this does not mean coaches can ignore learning. Just the opposite, in fact! All coaches need to be able to help teachers assess whether students are actually learning.

Achievement Data

Like most instructional coaches, Tamika spends a lot of her time working with teachers who are focused on improving student achievement. One such teacher is Courtney Bloom, a language arts teacher who has been teaching in the school for more than 20 years. Courtney is well known in the community because she ends each school year by choosing a famous poem for each of her students, writing the poem out by hand on a card, and handing each card out as a way to remember the class. Courtney frequently encounters students she taught 10, 15, or 20 years earlier who tell her that they still have their poetry card after all that time.

Courtney meets with Tamika to set a goal. Courtney has watched a video that Tamika recorded of one of her lessons, but her real concern is that her students are not writing effectively and don't seem interested in getting any better. "These kids need to understand that their ideas have to come out of their heads to make a difference," she says.

Although educators can gather data on achievement in many different ways, almost all approaches involve (1) unwrapping the standards (clarifying the knowledge, skills, and big ideas students need to learn); (2) describing learning goals (breaking down the knowledge, skills, and big ideas into precise, discrete statements); (3) breaking down the learning (determining how to gather data on whether students have learned what they need to learn); and (4) assessing student learning (adapting teaching and learning when the data show students aren't learning what they need to be learning). Together, Tamika and Courtney deal with all four elements of gathering data for achievement.

Unwrapping the Standards

Assessing achievement begins with identifying what students need to learn. In the United States, that usually involves taking a deep dive into state or Common Core standards. Larry Ainsworth, author of *"Unwrapping" the Common Core* (2015) and several other texts describing how to unwrap standards, suggests educators break down standards line by line and circle the nouns, which usually describe knowledge, and the verbs, which usually involve skills.

Ainsworth and others (e.g., Erickson & Tomlinson, 2007; Wiggins & McTighe, 2005) also recommend that educators look beyond knowledge and skills as they plan curriculum and identify the big ideas students need to learn in a course, unit, or lesson. "Big ideas" are usually concepts, principles, patterns, or themes.

Courtney wants her students to develop a deep understanding of the writing process, so she and Tamika decide to unpack the following 7th grade Common Core standard related to the writing process[1]:

> CCSS.ELA-Literacy.W.7.5. With some guidance and support from peers and adults, develop and strengthen writing as needed by planning, revising,

---

[1] I'm grateful to my colleague Sharon Thomas, who originally unpacked these standards for our workshop Instructional Coaching and Achievement.

editing, rewriting, or trying a new approach, focusing on how well purpose and audience have been addressed. (Editing for conventions should demonstrate command of Language Standards 1–3 up to and including grade 7 here.)

Going through the standard together, Courtney and Tamika identify *planning, revising, editing, rewriting, trying new approaches, purpose,* and *audience* as the knowledge students need to learn, and *planning, revising, editing, rewriting,* and *trying new approaches* as the skills students need to learn. Courtney feels that the overlap between knowledge and skills shows students need to both *know* and be able to *do* the writing process. "It's not enough that they can describe how to plan," Courtney says. "They actually have to do it, too." Courtney also identifies the big ideas she wants students to learn, including "writing to make a difference," "writing with purpose in mind," "writing as a form of self-expression," and "everyone can be a writer."

Describing Learning Goals

After Courtney and Tamika have identified the knowledge, skills, and big ideas students need to learn, they create guiding questions (as described in my book *High-Impact Instruction* [Knight, 2013]) so that students can see what they are going to learn. Together, they create six questions for the writing process based on the standard that describes what students need to learn in the unit:

1. What strategies can be used to plan writing?
2. What difference does writing make?
3. Why is it true that everyone can become a writer?
4. What is the writing process, and how can I edit, revise, rewrite, and try new approaches to improve writing?
5. Why is writing with the audience in mind important? What strategies can writers use to do this?
6. How can writing be used as a form of self-expression? Why is this important?

Breaking Down the Learning

After identifying the guiding questions, Tamika asks Courtney to answer them. Acting as Courtney's "secretary," Tamika then writes down several simple sentences that provide partial answers to the guiding questions. I refer to these specific and assessable segments as *specific proficiencies*. (Ten or more specific proficiencies may be needed to answer one guiding question.) A specific proficiency states in exact terms what students need to know, do, or understand to correctly answer a guiding question. Therefore, the easiest way to craft specific proficiencies is to answer the question "What knowledge do students need to know, what skills do they need to be able to demonstrate, and what concepts or principles do they need to understand to answer this question satisfactorily?"

The following are seven specific proficiencies Courtney identified for the first guiding question she and Tamika developed.

Guiding question: *What strategies can be used to plan writing?*
- Planning involves getting ideas out of your head.
- Planning involves organizing ideas.
- Brainstorming is writing down all the ideas you can think of about a topic.
- Clustering is doodling with bubbles to get ideas out of your head.
- Free writing is writing nonstop for five minutes or more.
- Ideas can be organized by using a planning map, frame, or other tool.
- Planning and organizing make writing more coherent.

Next, Courtney organizes the proficiencies into the sequence in which they will be learned. Larry Ainsworth (2015) refers to this sequencing as a "learning progression." When formatively assessed, specific proficiencies help teachers pinpoint where student learning has broken down. When teachers precisely understand students' roadblocks to learning, they know what feedback they need to provide to students, what changes they need to make to students' learning experiences, what adaptations they need to make to their instruction, and what (if any) content they need to reteach.

Assessing Student Learning

Once the standards are unwrapped, guiding questions are written, and specific proficiencies are identified, Tamika and Courtney discuss how to assess student learning.

Tests

Selected-response tests such as fill-in-the-blank, true-or-false, and multiple-choice or short-answer tests can yield valuable insight into whether students are learning.

Checks for understanding

One of the easiest and most powerful ways to assess student learning is to use checks for understanding, such as bell work, response cards, whiteboards, exit tickets, and so forth. One of the advantages of checks for understanding is that they can be used at any time during a lesson. You can download a list of sample checks for understanding at www.instructionalcoaching.com/bookstore/the-definitive-guide-to-instructional-coaching.

Courtney uses a T-chart like the one in Figure 5.4 to identify which checks for understanding she can use as formative assessments for her specific proficiencies.

Rubrics

Tamika knows that tests and checks for understanding are effective ways of assessing students' knowledge. But as she explains to Courtney, they are much less effective at measuring students' *skills*. To do that, she probably needs to use rubrics. In their *Introduction to Rubrics* (2005), Dannelle Stevens and Antonia Levi define a rubric as follows:

> At its most basic, a rubric is a scoring tool that lays out the specific expectations for an assignment. Rubrics divide an assignment into its component parts and provide a detailed description of what constitutes acceptable or unacceptable levels of performance for each of those parts. (p. 3)

Susan Brookhart (2013) distinguishes between two categories of rubrics. Analytic rubrics, she says, "describe work on each criterion separately" (p. 6). Holistic rubrics, by contrast, "describe the work by applying all the criteria at the same time and enabling an overall judgment of the quality of the work" (p. 6).

FIGURE 5.4	
Proficiency Assessment Form	
Example	
Specific Proficiency	**Assessment**
Planning involves getting ideas out of your head.	Exit ticket
Planning involves organizing ideas.	Whiteboards
Brainstorming is writing down all the ideas you can think of about a topic.	Response cards
Clustering is doodling with bubbles to get ideas out of your head.	Whiteboards
Free writing is writing nonstop for five minutes or more.	Bell work
Ideas can be organized by using a planning map, frame, or other tool.	Group answers
Planning and organizing make writing more coherent.	Exit ticket

Tamika focuses her attention on different forms of assessment that allow for an analytic assessment of student work or performance. She also uses assessment tools that belong to what Brookhart (2013) refers to as the "family of rubrics." Each is described below.

Checklists. Checklists, like the one shown in Figure 5.5, are effective tools for assessing something simple or discrete enough that it can be measured by a yes or no answer. Thus, checklists are excellent for assessing whether students have completed some part of an assignment or a process. If one item on a checklist is "Begin your paragraph with a topic sentence," that's not an assessment of the quality of the topic sentence; instead, it simply assesses whether a topic sentence begins the paragraph.

FIGURE 5.5	
Sample Checklist for the Writing Process	
Example	✅
Did I use strategies (such as brain dump, clustering, free writing) to get ideas out of my head?	◯
Did I use strategies (such as planning maps, the Frame, orderly notes) to organize my ideas?	◯
Did I write about a topic that I care about?	◯
Did I shape my writing to speak to a particular audience?	◯
Did I use editing strategies (such as C.O.P.S., nontranslatable words, Twitter test, active voice) to make my writing clearer?	◯
Did my writing express my chosen voice?	◯

Single-point rubrics (SPRs). Jennifer Gonzalez, who writes the blog *Cult of Pedagogy* (www.cultofpedagogy.com), has popularized the use of single-point rubrics, or SPRs. This form of assessment includes a single criterion at the center of the rubric, with space on either side for someone (teacher, student, or peer) to add comments related to areas for improvement and evidence of exceeding standards. On her website, Gonzalez (2015) lists three advantages of these simple rubrics:

- Teachers find them easier and faster to create. . . .
- Students find them easier to read when preparing an assignment. . . .
- They allow for higher-quality feedback, because teachers must specify key problem areas and notable areas of excellence for that particular student, rather than choosing from a list of generic descriptions.

A sample SPR is shown in Figure 5.6.

Multi-point rubrics (MPRs). Another option is the multi-point rubric, which involves breaking down different levels of accomplishment or performance. Often, each criterion of a rubric is described at different levels with words such as *beginning, developing, accomplished,* or *exemplary.* Effective MPRs communicate what a product or process should look like after it has been learned (see Figure 5.7).

FIGURE 5.6

Single-Point Rubric: The Writing Process

Areas for Improvement	Criteria	Strengths
	Planning Addresses all elements of the prompt	
	Revising Uses appropriate vocabulary throughout	
	Editing Conforms to conventions of standard English	
	Rewriting Uses transitions appropriately	
	New Approaches Teacher allows students to experiment with writing in different ways	

Courtney can use rubrics to grade student work, assigning different grades based on level of performance. Because rubrics are often most helpful for formative assessment, teachers can share them with students to provide feedback on performance. Students can also use rubrics to self-assess their work or to provide peer feedback. Once students understand rubrics, they better understand what they need to learn and how well they are learning.

Rubrics can be difficult to create at first. It is challenging to try to describe success criteria precisely and clearly. However, that is exactly why rubrics

FIGURE 5.7

Multi-Point Rubric

Score	4	3	2	1	0
Planning	Addresses all elements of the prompt	Addresses most elements of the prompt	Addresses some elements of the prompt	Addresses the prompt minimally if at all	There is no response, or the response is inappropriate.
	Clearly demonstrates attention to task and purpose and chooses evidence, organization, level of language, and writing style according to that task and purpose	Mostly demonstrates attention to task and purpose and chooses most evidence, organization, level of language, and writing style according to that task and purpose	Demonstrates some attention to task and purpose and chooses some evidence, organization, level of language, and writing style according to the needs of that audience	Demonstrates little to no attention to task and purpose and does not appear to choose evidence, organization, level of language, and writing style according to that task and purpose	
	Clearly demonstrates attention to audience and chooses evidence, organization, level of language, and writing style according to the needs of that audience	Mostly demonstrates attention to audience and chooses most evidence, organization, level of language, and writing style according to the needs of that audience	Demonstrates some attention to audience and chooses some evidence, organization, level of language, and writing style according to the needs of that audience	Demonstrates little to no attention to audience and does not appear to choose evidence, organization, level of language, and writing style according to the needs of that audience	

Revising	Consistently uses appropriate grade-level academic and general vocabulary throughout the piece Consistently maintains purpose and focus throughout the piece	Uses mostly appropriate grade-level academic and general vocabulary throughout the piece Mostly maintains purpose and focus throughout the piece	Uses some appropriate grade-level academic and general vocabulary throughout the piece Maintains some purpose and focus throughout the piece	Uses little to no appropriate grade-level academic and general vocabulary throughout the piece Maintains little to no purpose and focus throughout the piece	There is no response, or the response is inappropriate.
Editing	Consistently conforms to the conventions of standard written English Language and syntax are consistently clear and coherent.	Mostly conforms to the conventions of standard written English Language and syntax are mostly clear and coherent.	Sometimes conforms to the conventions of standard written English Language and syntax are sometimes clear and coherent.	Does not conform to the conventions of standard written English Language and syntax are not clear and coherent.	There is no response, or the response is inappropriate.
Rewriting	Consistently uses transitions appropriately between paragraphs and between sections of text	Mostly uses transitions appropriately between paragraphs and between sections of text	Sometimes uses transitions appropriately between paragraphs and between sections of text	Does not use transitions appropriately between paragraphs and between sections of text	There is no response, or the response is inappropriate.
Trying New Approaches	[Not assessed via writing tasks but necessary to include in instruction so that students have the tools to complete writing tasks independently]				

are so important. Creating rubrics deepens our knowledge of the content we teach and the outcomes we expect for our students. And when we understand our content better, our teaching and feedback become more effective, meaning that our students learn more.

Teaching Data

In her work as an instructional coach, Tamika also gathers data that show how teachers teach. Unlike engagement and achievement data, teaching data are usually not used to develop a PEERS goal since they don't meet the *student-focused* criterion. But they are still important.

Coaches gather data about instruction so teachers can see how they are implementing new strategies and whether they need to change their teaching. The teaching data that Tamika gathers include ratio of interaction, teacher talk versus student talk, questions, opportunities to respond, and instructional versus noninstructional time. Each is described in the following sections.

Ratio of Interaction

Ratio of interaction measures how teachers direct their attention to students. As student behavior expert Randy Sprick explains in his presentations and publications, students want to get their teacher's attention. "Imagine that every time you're giving students your attention, you're handing them a five-dollar bill," he says. "Now think about when you give students that bill. Is it because of appropriate or inappropriate behavior?" Randy's message is clear: if students are getting their teacher's attention by acting up, they'll keep acting up.

Tamika gathers data on ratio of interaction the same way she gathers many other forms of data: by using the class seating chart. When a teacher gives a student attention for appropriate behavior, she simply puts a plus under the student's name on the chart. When a teacher corrects the student, she puts down a minus. Sometimes she will note disruptions on the chart by using a third symbol for disruptive behavior.

Teacher Talk Versus Student Talk

One thing teachers often see when they watch video of their lessons is that they talk too much and students don't talk enough. This is an important discovery, because whoever is doing the talking is usually doing the learning (Clinton, Cairns, McLaren, & Simpson, 2014). Tamika gathers data on student talk by using her smartphone to keep track of when students talk and then subtracting that amount of time from the total class time.

Questions

One of the easiest and most powerful steps teachers can take to increase student engagement, and consequently learning, is to change the way they ask questions. Open questions entail a potentially infinite number of responses, and they usually elicit longer answers. Closed questions, by contrast, have a finite number of answers. A closed question might be "Who was the original voice of Darth Vader?" whereas an open question might be "Why do you think *Star Wars* movies are so popular?"

A second distinction is between right-or-wrong questions and opinion questions. Right-or-wrong questions, as the term implies, have right or wrong answers. Thus, a right-or-wrong question might be "What year was the first *Star Wars* movie released?" An opinion question, however, is one you can't get wrong, such as "Who is your favorite *Star Wars* character?"

Finally, a third distinction relates to the level of the questions. Many educators use Bloom's taxonomy to distinguish between levels. Other ways of sorting levels of questions include Lorin Anderson and David Krathwohl's (2001) revised version of Bloom, Robert Marzano's taxonomy (2001), and Norman Webb's Depth of Knowledge levels (2002). In our work at ICG, we sort questions into three levels: (1) knowledge, (2) skills, and (3) big ideas.

Tamika finds that what matters most with questioning is asking the right kind of question for the kind of learning that is taking place. She sorts learning into two categories: closed learning, during which students are expected to master content as it is directly taught, and open learning, during which students construct their own understandings.

For closed learning, teachers should generally ask a lot of closed, right-or-wrong questions, since a major purpose of questioning during closed learning is to confirm that students can demonstrate their understanding of the content as the teacher intends.

For open learning, where students construct their own understandings, open opinion questions are usually more effective, especially for promoting classroom conversation, because learners, whether young or older, usually hesitate to answer closed questions for fear of answering incorrectly in front of their peers. Open questions also usually provoke longer answers.

Opportunities to Respond

Opportunities to respond (OTR) refers to the number of different times students are prompted to react to what they are learning. Teachers create opportunities to respond by asking questions, directing students to turn to their neighbor and compare answers to a question, asking students to hold up response cards, and so forth.

Tamika gathers data on opportunities to respond on a seating chart by putting a tally under students' names when they are prompted to respond or by putting a tally on the side of the page when the class responds together to a prompt (e.g., in the case of choral responses to a question).

Opportunities to respond are most useful during direct instruction or closed learning, when frequent interactions increase engagement and learning. During open learning, a smaller number of questions promotes deeper thought and dialogue.

Instructional Versus Noninstructional Time

Noninstructional time refers to all the unproductive activities that occur in class, such as talking after the bell before class begins, lining up to leave the room before the bell rings, moving from one center to the next, handing out assignments, taking attendance, and so forth. Noninstructional time may also be referred to as *transition* or *wasted* time.

Some of the time students spend in any class is inevitably noninstructional. At the same time, it's obvious that the more time students spend on productive experiences, the more they are likely to learn. Tamika records instructional and noninstructional time the same way she records teacher and student talk.

Another way to measure instructional time is to note how much time is spent on various instructional or learning activities during a lesson. Tamika can display these data using a pie chart like the one shown in Figure 5.8 so teachers can immediately see how they are using their time during teaching.

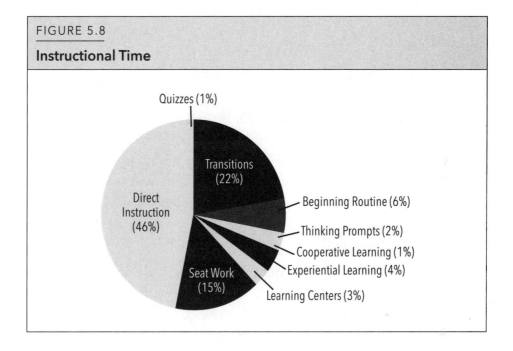

FIGURE 5.8

Instructional Time

As an instructional coach, Tamika gathers data almost every day to help teachers set goals, measure progress, make adaptations, or look at how teaching strategies are being implemented. Data serve as a GPS for the learning journey students take in school. But data only measure the impact of changes: teachers and coaches still need teaching strategies so that students can meet goals. That is why Tamika, like all instructional coaches, needs an instructional playbook that describes the high-impact teaching strategies she most frequently shares with teachers. In Chapter 6, you'll learn what any coach can do to create such a playbook.

To Sum Up

When possible, data should be

- Chosen by the teacher;
- Objective;
- Gathered frequently;
- Valid;
- Reliable and mutually understood; and
- Gathered by teachers.

Engagement should be a focus for instructional coaching because it is an essential part of a fulfilling life and the main reason why students stay in school. Coaches and teachers can gather behavioral, cognitive, and emotional engagement data.

Of course, achievement should also be central to instructional coaching. To assess achievement, coaches and teachers must clarify what students need to learn by unpacking standards, creating guiding questions, and developing specific proficiencies. Achievement can be measured with tests, checks for understanding, and both single- and multi-point rubrics.

Reflection Questions

1. To what extent are data a part of my coaching?
2. What are the most common types of goals I set with teachers, and what data do I gather to monitor progress toward those goals? Do I need to change anything about the data I gather?
3. How confident am I that my data are reliable? Do I partner with colleagues to ensure that my data collection is reliable?
4. Do I agree that data should be objective rather than subjective? Why or why not?
5. Do I agree that data should be gathered frequently? Why or why not?
6. What can I do to ensure that the data I gather are valid?
7. Do I agree that instructional coaching should address both engagement and achievement? Why or why not?
8. What can I do to make it possible for teachers to gather their own data?

Going Deeper

- I first started to understand the power of data after partnering with Randy Sprick and Wendy Reinke in 2005 to explore coaching and classroom management. Together with Tricia Skyles and Lynn Barnes, we wrote *Coaching Classroom Management* (Sprick, Knight, Reinke, Skyles, & Barnes, 2006). I've been learning from all of my coauthors since then.

- The classic book on data and coaching is Nancy Love, Katherine Stiles, Susan Mundry, and Kathryn DiRanna's *The Data Coach's Guide to Improving Learning for All Students* (2008). Other excellent books on data include Laura Lipton and Bruce Wellman's *Got Data? Now What?* (2012) and Kathryn Parker Boudet, Elizabeth City, and Richard Murnane's *Data Wise* (2005).

- Phil Schlechty's *Engaging Students* (2011) deepened my understanding of engagement. My favorite book on the topic is *Engagement by Design* (2018) by Doug Fisher, Nancy Frey, Russ Quaglia, Dominique Smith, and Lisa Lande.

- There are many books about curriculum planning, but I've been particularly influenced by Larry Ainsworth and Donald Viegut's *Common Formative Assessments 2.0* (2014), Grant Wiggins and Jay McTighe's *Understanding by Design* (2005), and Jan Chappuis and Rick Stiggins's *An Introduction to Student-Involved Assessment for Learning* (2017).

- Finally, my book *High-Impact Instruction* (2013) goes into more detail about many of the ideas in this chapter.

What's Next?

This chapter is packed with information about data. I suggest coaches review all the suggested types of engagement and achievement data and the corresponding measures, then identify which data they will make a part of their coaching. Coaches need to make sure they have a clear understanding of each type of data and the various ways it can be measured. There is great value in creating T-charts that describe what a concept or measure is and is not. Finally, coaches should visit classrooms together, gather data, and share notes until their observations are reliable. Coaches can also learn a lot from watching videos of teachers, gathering data from the videos independently, and then going through each video minute by minute, discussing the finer points of data gathering.

Learning Map for Chapter 6

The Instructional Playbook

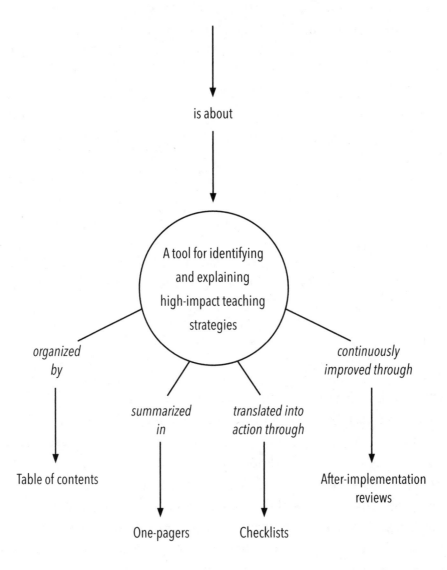

is about

A tool for identifying and explaining high-impact teaching strategies

organized by

summarized in

translated into action through

continuously improved through

Table of contents

One-pagers

Checklists

After-implementation reviews

6 The Instructional Playbook

If you can't explain it simply, you don't understand it well enough.

—Albert Einstein (in Lefever, *The Art of Explanation*)

April Strong is an instructional coach in Martin County School District in Florida. When I first spoke with April, she had been in education for 13 years. She spent the first 10 years teaching 4th and 5th grades, but she had set the goal for herself that after teaching for 10 years, she would shift to supporting teachers. "I had been supported so much by my peers," she said, "and I wanted to give something back to the profession that I love so much." In her 10th year, April was hired as an instructional coach.

When I talked with April about her use of an instructional playbook, she told me about working with David Yankwitt, a second-year social studies teacher. At first, she was anxious about partnering with him. She didn't know David, who had been told to work with her because his students' scores on the district benchmark assessments were low. April knew coaching went more smoothly when she worked with teachers who volunteered for coaching. She also was nervous that it might pose a problem that she was an elementary teacher and David was a secondary teacher. "I tried not to let the secondary teachers know I was an elementary teacher," she said, "but you can smell it all over me."

To her relief, David was interested in coaching. "Right away, he was very open about needing help and didn't put on a show. He admitted there was a lot to do, and we hit the ground running." "Thank goodness you're here!" David exclaimed, making April feel like a "lifeline."

David had a lot to learn. "He was doing the typical stand-and-deliver instructional strategy and getting very little engagement from his students," said April. As a result, he and April quickly turned their focus to engagement. April introduced David to a lot of Kagan cooperative learning strategies (Kagan & Kagan, 2009), like the Carousel strategy and Graffiti on the Wall. "We tried a lot of things to get the kids up and moving," April said. "David ultimately liked using technology strategies and self-paced questioning and answering, like [the learning game] Kahoot! and quizzes." David also started using turn-and-talk and other groupings. Students were assigned roles in groups and followed the round robin strategy. "David worked on moving kids from one station to the next and having conversations," April explained.

As David became more skilled, he saw success and started to become more confident as a teacher. "He recognized the importance of intentional planning and rooting [instruction] in the standards in different ways," April explained. The strategies David used translated into results. In one shot, his class's overall percentage on the district assessment went from 62 percent to 83 percent.

When David texted April the wonderful results, she "squealed and did a little bit of a happy dance," she said. "I am his biggest fan, and I celebrated how hard he worked and what he was able to do with students." What was most gratifying to April was David's desire to keep learning. "He's feeling the power of learning and growing professionally, the power of working with me as a partner."

A year after David had gotten the great test results, I contacted April to fact-check this chapter. She told me that the story wasn't over: the week before, David informed her that he had won Social Studies Teacher of the Year for the district.

What Is an Instructional Playbook?

April was able to help David because she had a deep understanding of teaching strategies that would help him increase student engagement. Once David learned those practices, he succeeded. The teaching strategies April shared were not simply good ideas that she had picked up along the way. She knew the strategies well because she had a tool that prepared her to succeed as an instructional coach: the instructional playbook. As my colleagues Ann Hoffman, Michelle Harris, Sharon Thomas, and I explain in *The Instructional Playbook* (2020), anyone who aspires to be an effective instructional coach needs an instructional playbook.

Part of what prompted us to write that book was our discovery that many coaches cannot name the teaching strategies they share with teachers or are unclear about how the strategies they share are to be effectively implemented. Since the job of an instructional coach is to support teachers as they try to get better, coaches need to understand—and understand well—the strategies they share.

Playbooks are essential because they make learning real. Far too often, we pretend professional development will have a positive impact on what takes place in classrooms when we know that, in reality, usually nothing will happen after the event. A presenter might offer an entertaining and interesting workshop, but unless the participants do the hard work of deeply understanding strategies and how to use them, they won't implement them. The shelves in teachers' classrooms around the world are filled with books that were never opened once the workshop was over. Instructional playbooks are designed to change that by empowering coaches and teachers to take research off the shelf and put it into action in the classroom.

In short, instructional playbooks are organizational tools that professional developers use to (1) identify high-impact teaching strategies and (2) explain those strategies to teachers so they and their students can meet powerful goals. Instructional playbooks are essential because too often, teachers don't have the specific, practical information they need to implement teaching strategies effectively, even after reading books or attending professional development sessions. Like all professionals, teachers need ideas to be translated into explicit, actionable knowledge if they are going to implement them. As April Strong explains, "The instructional playbook brings clarity by breaking things down, step by step, to make an impact on how our teachers are instructing our students."

Why We Need Instructional Playbooks

In preparation for our book *The Instructional Playbook* (Knight et al., 2020), ICG researcher Geoff Knight and I interviewed many educators who are creating and using instructional playbooks. Following are several reasons why coaches said they needed this tool.

Instructional Playbooks Help Identify the Highest-Impact Teaching Strategies

In many schools, too many teaching strategies are being promoted at the same time. The reason is understandable: educators and their students face many challenges, and leaders feel a duty to try to provide solutions. Unfortunately, as one strategy is piled on after another, many teachers and coaches start to feel overwhelmed. As a result, rather than helping, adding more and more strategies to a teacher's already busy schedule can end up making things worse. Even though the programs and strategies that teachers and coaches are learning are likely powerful and effective, no one can implement all of them, and having too many innovations can lead to overload and poor implementation. Faced with the impossible task of trying to learn and use too many new strategies, educators may settle for superficial implementation just to show they are compliant with their leaders' wishes and thereby fail to implement the strategies in ways that help students.

One of the most important features of the instructional playbook is that it forces coaches and leaders to identify the highest-impact strategies among the many they are often confronted with. We suggest that a playbook contain no more than 15 to 20 strategies. If you can't list all your teaching strategies on a single page, you have too many. The high-impact strategies in the playbook are not the only ones coaches share or co-construct with teachers, but they are the core of their work on instruction. Once coaches have identified the most important strategies, they can focus on developing the deep understanding necessary to support effective professional learning.

Instructional Playbooks Lead to Deep Understanding

As I've been writing this book, my soundtrack has been Zhu Xiao-Mei's Bach recordings. Listening to this music has been a joyful part of many writing sessions. At the same time, Zhu Xiao-Mei has been teaching me about deep understanding. In her book *The Secret Piano* (2007), she explains that one of her first teachers, Pan Yiming, taught her to memorize each piece she plays. "I want you to play all of this by heart," he told her. "From now on, for each lesson, you must play a piece by Bach and two études from memory and with no mistakes. Try to memorize each of them from the very first time that you sight-read them" (p. 38).

"Easy for him to say" (p. 38), Zhu Xiao-Mei thought—but in the end, she took his advice. Throughout her book, the pianist explains all the ways she comes to deeply understand a piece. She explores, memorizes, meditates, and immerses herself in the music, she says, until "I experience love for each passage and note, until I reach a state of natural and intuitive understanding.... By living with a piece, by not attempting to impose yourself in any way, you begin to breathe with it" (p. 222). And when you watch Zhu Xiao-Mei perform Bach's "Goldberg Variations," playing it with her eyes closed so that she can feel every note more deeply, you get to see and hear deep understanding in action.

Similarly, coaches need to live with the teaching strategies they share to deeply understand their nuances. What coaches say about strategies will affect what teachers do, so if their explanations are superficial or incorrect, teachers' practice will likely be ineffective. Coaches need to offer high-quality explanations to foster high-quality implementation.

Instructional Playbooks Unblock Barriers to Deep Understanding

Four issues in particular interfere with our ability to develop deep understanding.

First, we may get a wide but shallow understanding of effective instruction by trying to learn too much too fast. When coaches try to learn everything, they may find that when it comes to precise, practical knowledge, they really haven't learned *anything*.

Second, we may persuade ourselves that we know things better than we do. Michael Fullan (1982) refers to this as "false clarity"—a tendency to be totally confident in our incorrect understandings of practices. I've watched video of many instructional coaches whose explanations of teaching strategies are confident, clear—and wrong. (Unfortunately, I myself have been on many of those videos.)

A third issue involves a way of knowing that is the opposite of false clarity. Sometimes we know strategies so well that our knowledge actually makes it hard for us to explain them. Colin Camerer, George Loewenstein, and Martin Weber (1989) describe this as the "curse of knowledge," which occurs when we have internalized so much information that we forget what we had to go through to learn it. As Heath and Heath (2007) explain, "Once we know something, we find it hard to imagine what it was like not to know it. Our knowledge has cursed us. And it becomes difficult for us to share our knowledge with others because we can't readily re-create our listeners' state of mind" (p. 20).

Finally, a fourth roadblock to deep understanding is a phenomenon I call the "curse of forgetting." Sometimes during explanations, coaches simply forget to explain important parts of strategies. Fortunately, creating and using an instructional playbook helps coaches circumvent all four of these roadblocks to deep understanding.

Instructional Playbooks Build a Shared Vocabulary

When educators come together to create a playbook, they often discover that they don't have shared definitions for terms that they use all the time. Vague definitions of terms can create the illusion of harmony. If I define *engagement* in my way and you define it in yours, even if we both agree that engagement is important, we aren't really agreeing because we don't know what the other person means by the term.

Real, shared understanding requires deep understanding. The collaborative conversations needed to create the playbook produce a shared, precise understanding of terms and strategies that is essential for meaningful conversation. True communication is only possible when people know what each other's words mean.

Instructional Playbooks Improve the Quality of Conversations About Teaching

One theme my colleagues and I have heard across many interviews with coaches is that the deep understanding that comes from creating instructional playbooks improves the quality of conversations about teaching. For example, Maureen Hill, an instructional coach, related that "just kind of working on [the playbook] and creating one-pagers and checklists has helped bring clarity to conversations—just being more specific in what we are trying to fix and work on because I have to be clear and concise when I explain teaching strategies."

Similarly, Mary Webb, who directs the coaching program in the Frisco Independent School District, told us that one of the advantages of the playbook is that it increases clarity. "When I use the checklists from the playbook, I'm able to clearly communicate what a strategy looks like for teachers. So when teachers implement a strategy, there's no room for them not to understand because the checklist is so clear, and I'm able to communicate so clearly. If you are using the checklists from the playbook, you're removing a lot of error from communication."

Instructional Playbooks Reduce Stress

Because instructional coaching is a relatively new position in many educational settings, coaches report that one of the most stressful aspects of their job is a lack of clarity. Too many aren't clear on what they are expected to do, what success looks like for them, or even how they will be evaluated. Additionally, many coaches aren't that clear on the actual teaching practices they are supposed to share.

This kind of ambiguity can lead to cognitive overload. When coaches try to remember everything, they can get overwhelmed. As Joi Lunsford, an instructional coach in Amarillo, Texas, told us, "You can only hold so much information."

For these reasons, one of the most important advantages of using an instructional playbook is that coaches feel less ambiguity and, therefore, less stress.

Instructional Playbooks Foster Hope

As I've mentioned before in this book, hope involves three factors: a goal, pathways to the goal, and agency (a belief that we can hit the goal) (Lopez, 2013). The instructional playbook gives coaches the resources they need to help teachers see pathways to their goals. In a well-designed playbook, every high-impact teaching strategy listed should be extremely effective at helping teachers meet goals. When teachers see the pathway to their goal made possible by effective strategies, they begin to have hope.

Who Creates the Playbook?

The instructional playbook is created by a playbook development team. The team may include school administrators, curriculum leaders, teachers, students, and others, but, most important, it must be made up of the coaches who will be sharing the playbook and the person who directs the coaching program.

Usually, decisions about team membership are made by the director of the coaching program. The more people on the team, the greater an understanding there will be about the teaching practices that coaches make a priority. At the same time, having more people increases the challenges placed on the facilitator and the time it takes to produce the final product.

To get around this issue, some school districts have different-sized teams for different parts of the playbook creation process. Thus, a team might be quite inclusive and large at the beginning of the process, when the playbook's table of contents is being created and high-impact strategies are being identified, but be much smaller, and consequently more efficient, when checklists are being developed.

Leaders might be tempted to simply create the playbook that their coaches will use, but the people we interviewed said they felt the playbook should be created with others. "I really wanted to do it by myself, just because I wanted to get it done," said Amber Theinel. "But there's no way. I could never have done this by myself. So definitely don't do it alone."

Some local customization of the playbook may be necessary, with different settings requiring different strategies. For example, if one school has all teachers with at least 15 years' experience and hardly any students on free or reduced lunch, while another school has only teachers with fewer than 4 years' experience and 95 percent of students on free or reduced lunch, the coaches at those two schools will likely need different strategies. It makes no sense for coaches to have playbooks that don't help teachers in their school meet their goals.

Nevertheless, to the greatest extent possible, playbooks should be consistent. When all coaches have similar strategies in their playbooks, professional development can be offered for everyone, and by working from a shared understanding of strategies, coaches will have better conversations about the strategies they are using.

Contents of the Instructional Playbook

An instructional playbook is a deceptively simple document made up of three sections:

1. A table of contents

2. "One-pagers"

3. Checklists

Of course, each team can add or remove whatever sections it wants in order to create its own unique playbook. But I caution everyone to keep it simple. If the playbook is too complex, it may end up sitting on a shelf rather than being used by coaches with teachers.

Table of Contents

The table of contents is a list of teaching strategies that takes up no more than one page and functions, as you might guess, as an outline for the instructional playbook. The strategies listed in the table of contents should all be proven and evidence-based and address most of the goals teachers have set. Most important, the strategies should effectively empower teachers and students to meet the goals teachers set for or with students. Figure 6.1 shows a sample table of contents.

The idea that the table of contents has to be one page long isn't etched in granite. Each team needs to create the right list for its setting. However, I have found that limiting the list to one page forces the team to think very deeply about each strategy on the page and why it must be there.

When creating a table of contents, teams can get bogged down if they fail to clarify the difference between strategies and activities. As a working definition, I refer to *strategies* as categories of teaching practices and *activities* as individual examples of those categories. For example, cooperative learning is a strategy that can involve many different activities. Those who are creating the table of contents will never fit the 100-plus activities or learning structures from Kagan and Kagan's *Kagan Cooperative Learning* (2009) on one page. But if they use the term *cooperative learning* in the table of contents, that term can refer to any number of student activities broadly categorized as part of cooperative learning.

In some settings, coaches might base their playbook on comprehensive instructional approaches that already exist, such as my book *High-Impact Instruction* (Knight, 2013); Jon Saphier, Mary Ann Haley-Speca, and Robert Gower's *The Skillful Teacher* (2017); Robert Marzano's *The New Art and Science of Teaching* (2017); or John Hattie's *Visible Learning for Teachers* (2009).

In other settings, the playbook can bring together diverse teaching strategies from a variety of sources, such as Randy Sprick's *CHAMPS* (2009); Janis Bulgren, Jean Schumaker, and Donald Deshler's *The Concept Mastery Routine* (1993); and Jan Chappuis and Rick Stiggins's *Introduction to Student-Involved Assessment for Learning* (2017).

FIGURE 6.1

Sample Table of Contents

Content Planning
- Guiding Questions
- Learning Maps

Formative Assessment
- Specific Proficiencies
- Checks for Understanding
- Rubrics
- Tests

Instruction
- Thinking Prompts
- Effective Questions
- Stories
- Cooperative Learning
- Authentic Learning

Community Building
- Culture
- Power With
- Freedom Within Form
- Expectations
- Witness to the Good
- Fluent Corrections

Whether sorting through teaching strategies from one specific instructional model or bringing together strategies from various resources, the team must still identify the specific strategies that will make it into the table of contents. To do this, start by listing the most common goals that teachers identify during coaching. Then, brainstorm all the strategies teachers could use to hit those goals. Next, reduce the identified strategies to a list that is both comprehensive (addressing all the common goals) and high-impact (made up of strategies that really work). After completing the list, sort the strategies into categories to make the list easier to understand. For example, in *High-Impact Instruction* (Knight, 2013), I sort teaching strategies into what I call "the Big Four": planning, assessment, instruction for engagement and mastery, and community building.

One-Pagers

The second section of the instructional playbook contains one-pagers—documents that are written for each strategy listed in the table of contents. As you might guess, the documents are one page in length. A well-designed one-pager provides a quick summary of important information about each strategy in the playbook.

Each one-pager begins with a single sentence that answers two questions: "What is this strategy?" and "What does it do?" This sentence should be crafted in simple, correct language that is easily understood (as should every sentence in the playbook). This sentence is followed by a summary of the research evidence that supports use of a given strategy. The discussions that team members have about research related to effective instruction while creating one-pagers can be an opportunity to develop a districtwide deeper understanding of research methods. The one-pager also contains a "What's the point?" section summarizing why and how the strategy should be used. Finally, two sections describe how the strategy is used by students and teachers.

Figure 6.2 shows an example of a one-pager for learning maps (much like the ones at the start of each chapter in this book). These maps help students to see the big picture of their learning and the connections between the things they're learning.

When ICG consultant Ann Hoffman leads teams that are creating one-pagers, she suggests a simple three-part process. First, everyone creates an individual draft of the one-pager. (The idea is that each team tackles one strategy at a time.) Next, everyone shares their version of the one-pager. Finally, the team determines the best way to synthesize all ideas.

In some cases, the team will need help to summarize the research. Some research is complex and difficult to understand, and researchers themselves often spend a great deal of time disagreeing about what data mean. But this doesn't mean that educators should ignore research. A better idea is to use research to identify high-impact strategies. Ultimately, the test of any strategy is how well it works to help students meet goals (which is why the after-implementation review meeting, described later in this chapter, is so important).

FIGURE 6.2

Sample One-Pager: Learning Maps

In One Sentence

A graphic organizer depicting the essential knowledge, skills, and big ideas students are to learn in a unit, used to organize students' learning and teachers' instruction.

What Research Says
- Hattie, *Visible Learning* (2008): Teacher Clarity ($d = .75$); Concept Mapping ($d = .75$)
- Marzano, Pickering, & Pollock, *Classroom Instruction That Works* (2001): Nonlinguistic Representations ($d = .75$)

What's the Point?
- Learning maps are powerful because their visual depiction of a unit keeps students and teachers on track.
- The map is an accommodation for students who struggle to take notes, and it structures the beginning and end of lessons.
- Learning maps are living study guides that make connections explicit and support repeated review.

How Are Learning Maps Used by Teachers?
- Teachers should spend 25 to 40 minutes to introduce the unit through an interactive discussion of the map on the first day of a unit.
- Throughout the unit, the maps may be used as visual prompts for conversations around advance and post-organizers.
- Teachers should prompt students to record new information on their maps as they learn it.
- At the end of the unit, maps may be integrated into the unit review.

How Are Learning Maps Used by Students?
Students use learning maps
- To take note of key information.
- To frequently review and clarify their learning.
- As points of departure for classroom dialogue.

Ultimately, the one-pager is a tool coaches use to clearly communicate with teachers about the strategies they may use in their classroom. Creating a one-pager deepens coaches' understanding of strategies. That clarity must be reflected in the accurate, precise, and easy-to-understand wording of the document. The playbook development team needs to keep working until each document it creates can be immediately understood.

Checklists

The bulk of an instructional playbook is made up of checklists. My colleagues and I at the University of Kansas Center for Research on Learning have been field-testing checklists for more than two decades. When we first began studying instructional coaching in 1996, we realized that our explanations had to be precise and actionable to be effective, and we learned that the easiest way to accomplish this was to structure our explanations around checklists.

Given our interest in checklists, we were thrilled to read Atul Gawande's *New York Times* best seller *The Checklist Manifesto* (2011). As he explains in a TED Talk, Gawande (2012) was as surprised as anyone that he ended up studying checklists. "I did not expect to be spending a significant part of my time as a Harvard surgeon worrying about checklists," he says. "And yet what we found [was] that these were tools to help make experts better."

In partnership with the World Health Organization, Gawande studied the impact of surgical checklists in eight hospitals around the world, deliberately choosing a wide range of settings, with four hospitals from wealthier countries (the United States, Canada, New Zealand, and England) and four from poorer countries (Tanzania, Jordan, India, and the Philippines). The results were stunning: when surgical teams used checklists, complication rates in all hospitals fell an average of 35 percent and death rates fell by 47 percent. Largely because of this research, checklists are now seen as essential to effective care in hospitals around the world. If you've visited a hospital recently, you've probably seen someone using a checklist.

We have found that checklists are just as important in the classroom as they are in the operating room. Checklists help coaches show teachers how to turn abstract concepts into actions. When conversations around teaching strategies are too abstract or general, teachers struggle to implement what's being discussed. For example, we might say that we want there to be more higher-order thinking in our classrooms, but remain unclear on what we actually need to do to make that happen. Conversations at the general level sound helpful, and they do provide an opportunity for exploring concepts, but they do not, on their own, lead to real change. The coaches we interviewed reported that they found that checklists helped them be more specific and consequently more effective.

Instructional coach Rachel LeForce explained that, for her, creating checklists was "kind of growing my own competency. I was making sure that I wasn't giving teachers fluff. I actually think that in providing rigor for myself, I have provided rigor for my teachers, and that is translating into rigor for our students."

To create checklists for the playbook, coaches need to think deeply about precisely what a teaching strategy involves and then identify a simple, clear way to say that. Indeed, one of the most important reasons for creating a checklist is simply to experience the deep understanding that results from that creative act. When coaches understand their strategies better, their explanations are clearer, teachers' implementation is more powerful, and student learning benefits.

A checklist is also a great communication tool. Because it is external to both the coach and the teacher, talking about it feels more collaborative than if the coach directly tells a teacher how to implement a strategy. The items on the checklist also provide a way for the coach to encourage teacher voice and deeper understanding at the same time. When coaches ask collaborating teachers if they want to modify a strategy for their students, teachers see that their voices count and learn more about the strategy because they have to understand it before they can change it.

Checklists can serve several purposes. Sometimes they are used to describe how to do something; for example, how to create learning maps. Other times they serve as rubrics for quality products (e.g., by identifying the characteristics of excellent learning maps). Checklists can also be used by coaches to describe what teachers or students do. For example, a coach might use one checklist to describe how teachers can use learning maps to introduce a day's lesson and a different one to describe how students use the maps to self-assess and prepare for tests.

A checklist should make it easy for teachers to implement a teaching strategy in a way that has an unmistakably positive impact on student learning or well-being. To accomplish this, checklists should be as short as possible without leaving out important information. Additionally, they should convey the key information about a strategy in precise, easy-to-understand language. (See Figure 6.3 for a checklist on how to use checklists.)

FIGURE 6.3	
Checklist for Checklists	
An effective checklist is . . .	✓
Concise—fewer than 10 lines and as short as possible	
Right—steps of the strategy are correctly described	
Precise—each item is clearly described	
Easy to understand—uses the right words stated in the simplest way	
Comprehensive—addresses everything that needs to be addressed	

When we partner with teams to facilitate the creation of checklists like the one depicted in Figure 6.4, we ask team members to review the publications that describe the teaching strategies they have included in their table of contents. Then, during the meeting, as we do with the one-pager, we ask everyone to draft individual checklists on their own. Following this, we guide the team to integrate and synthesize comments until a document is created that everyone, or almost everyone, accepts. After the meeting, a designated person edits the checklist to make it as simple, clear, and concise as possible before it is included in the playbook.

Not every teaching strategy requires a checklist. A coach who is working with a teacher on questioning, for example, probably doesn't need a checklist to distinguish between open and closed questions. And sometimes a coach and teacher will need to create a checklist together when they are working on a strategy that isn't in the coach's playbook. There is value in co-creating checklists, but we have found that creating a concise, actionable, powerful checklist takes more time than teachers usually have. When we create a checklist in advance and then go through it with the teacher to modify it so that it is a good fit for the teacher and students, we still experience co-creation while saving time.

FIGURE 6.4

Sample Checklist: The Cue, Do, Review Teaching Routine

TEACHER BEHAVIOR	✓
CUE	
Name the graphic organizer.	
Explain how it will help students learn.	
Specify what they need to do.	
DO	
Walk through the graphic organizer.	
Involve students.	
Shape student responses.	
Evaluate student understanding.	
Reinstruct if necessary.	
REVIEW	
Ask questions about information on the graphic organizer.	
Ask questions about how the graphic organizer works.	

Note: The Cue, Do, Review teaching routine appears in "Content Enhancement: A Model for Promoting the Acquisition of Content by Individuals with Learning Disabilities," by B. K. Lenz, J. A. Bulgren, and P. Hudson, in T. E. Scruggs and B. L. Y. Wong (Eds.), *Intervention Research in Learning Disabilities* (pp. 122–165), 1990, New York: Springer.

After-Implementation Review: Using the Playbook to Document Learning About Teaching

Many organizations use a learning process first developed by the U.S. Army called an after-action review, or AAR, to document the learning that occurs after an event. As explained in the *U.S. Army Leadership Field Manual* (Department of the Army, 2004), "An AAR is a professional discussion of an event, focused on performance standards, that allows participants to discover for themselves what happened, why it happened, and how to sustain strengths and improve on weaknesses" (p. 6). Discussion during the AAR is built around four questions:

1. What was supposed to happen?
2. What really happened?
3. What accounts for the difference?
4. What should we do differently next time?

This simple routine has now become an organizational learning process in thousands of organizations around the world.

Educators can use a similar procedure, which I refer to as the after-implementation review (AIR), to surface, synthesize, and document their learning about the strategies in the playbook. This review can occur formally, in a structured AIR meeting, or informally, during coaching meetings.

Both formal and informal AIRs give educators opportunities to discuss what they are learning about the strategies in the playbook and then revise the playbook to include what has been learned. Playbooks are living documents, where organizational learning about teaching and learning is synthesized and recorded. As Joi Lunsford, an instructional coach in Amarillo, Texas, said about her district's playbook, "I don't know if it will ever be complete. It is something that we are constantly editing, updating, and tweaking."

Instructional coaches are frontline learners who see what is and what isn't working with a given teaching practice. Each time a teacher sets a goal and implements a new strategy, that teacher's coach should be learning which teaching strategies are effective and how strategies should be modified to be more effective in each school's context.

PEERS goals (see pp. 91–92) provide a helpful, objective measuring stick for assessing the effectiveness of strategies. Instructional coaches who spend most of their time partnering with teachers to set and hit goals will be learning almost daily about which strategies work and how they work best. The AIR is the process for gathering all that learning before it is lost.

The Formal After-Implementation Review

At least twice a year, but preferably more frequently, coaches should meet with the coaching program director to carefully consider what is and is not working with the teaching strategies in the playbook. Formal discussion should be scheduled for a half-day to allow for careful assessment of all the strategies. While others may participate, those who have firsthand knowledge about the strategies and will be sharing them with teachers should be at the heart of the discussion about revising the playbook.

Participants should come to the AIR prepared to discuss their experiences using the strategies in the playbook. Each team member can prepare by writing down responses to each of the AIR questions shown on page 157. An agenda built around the AIR questions should be distributed at least a week before the meeting.

The meeting itself should be led by a skilled facilitator who listens effectively, encourages everyone to participate, keeps the discussion moving, and makes sure that a few voices do not dominate discussion. Further, the facilitator should not take sides during discussion and should ensure everyone is heard. For this reason, it may be helpful to have a facilitator who is neither a coach nor responsible for the coaching program.

Someone should be designated as note taker to document what is learned. Notes should be circulated as soon as possible after the meeting and filed so that they can be reviewed in a later meeting if necessary. Participants also need to understand how decisions are made—whether by the program director, a majority vote, a committee that meets after the AIR, or some other way. The simplest and perhaps most agreeable process is to go by majority vote. (When it comes to removing a strategy from the playbook, a two-thirds majority rule might be prudent to guard against prematurely removing a strategy that could prove to be effective in the future.)

I suggest the discussion be guided by the following AIR questions:

1. What's working with the strategies in the playbook?
2. What are we learning about the strategies in the playbook?
3. What refinements can be made to the strategies in the playbook?
4. What issues are not addressed but should be addressed by the strategies in the playbook?
5. What new strategies should we consider adding to the playbook?
6. What strategies either aren't working or aren't being used and thus should be removed from the playbook?
7. How well does the playbook align with district initiatives? Does the playbook need to change? Do district leaders need to hear anything about district initiatives?
8. What else can we do to make the playbook simpler or more useful?
9. What else should we do to improve the playbook?

What's working with the strategies in the playbook?

This first question provides a chance for everyone to revisit why the instructional playbook exists and what it is helping coaches accomplish. This component of the discussion also offers a chance for coaches to celebrate the difference they are making in students' and educators' lives.

What are we learning about the strategies in the playbook?

This is an open question designed to encourage everyone to share general experiences with the playbook. As they work with teachers, coaches learn a lot about the best ways to implement teaching strategies. This question presents an opportunity for everyone to start providing more specific feedback on coaches' experiences with the strategies in the playbook. All comments, both positive and negative, should be welcomed and noted.

What refinements can be made to the strategies in the playbook?

Coaches and teachers frequently adapt teaching strategies so that they better meet the needs of students or better fit a teacher's strengths or principles. For example, a teacher and coach might discover that it's important to review prior knowledge during the beginning of a teaching routine or that student behavior improves when students have a voice in setting community norms and expectations. Often, refinements are recorded on the checklists that teachers and coaches use for classroom instruction and learning.

Over time, all coaches should be learning better ways to implement the strategies in the playbook. Such refinements should be documented and shared, and one way for that to occur is during discussion of this question.

What issues are not addressed but should be addressed by the strategies in the playbook?

The perfect playbook would address every important issue for every student in every classroom. But there is no perfect playbook, which is why all of them need to be continually improved through the AIR.

One way to improve a playbook is to consider what PEERS goals the strategies are *not* addressing. After surfacing these issues, coaches can look to articles, books, conferences, institutes, workshops, experts, podcasts, blogs, and other resources to find teaching strategies that might help teachers and students meet more goals.

What new strategies should we consider adding to the playbook?

To get better at helping teachers meet PEERS goals, coaches need to be curators of knowledge. That is, they should be constantly deepening their understanding of the strategies they know while expanding their knowledge of other strategies that could improve how they help teachers and students meet goals. Coaches' deep understanding of teaching strategies is empowered by the creation of the playbook and is deepened by their day-to-day partnerships with teachers as teachers implement and learn about strategies.

Coaches should also be learning about new practices by reading journals and books, reviewing blogs and podcasts, and attending conferences, institutes, and workshops. Then, to establish local validity, coaches should share the highest-impact strategies they learn about with teachers. If the strategies help teachers help students meet goals, coaches should share them with their colleagues, and during the AIR, the team should consider whether the new strategies should replace other strategies or simply be added to the playbook.

What strategies either aren't working or aren't being used?

In their collaborative work with teachers, coaches will discover that some teaching strategies are not as effective as anticipated when teachers actually implement them. Additionally, there may be strategies in the playbook that, despite their promise, never get used. If a strategy has been in a playbook for a year without anybody using it, or if a strategy in the playbook has been found not to help teachers or students, it should be removed so that a higher-impact strategy can be included instead.

How well does the playbook align with district initiatives?

Most districts invest in professional development to address important issues in schools. Frequently, a coach's responsibilities include helping teachers learn and effectively implement the practices shared during professional development.

To prioritize their time effectively, coaches need guidance from their district leaders on how to align their coaching work on PEERS goals with the implementation support they provide for districtwide strategies. For all the reasons stated in earlier chapters of this book, the best scenario is that the strategies promoted at the district level are highly effective at helping teachers meet PEERS goals. When this isn't the case, coaches should have an opportunity to discuss their experiences with strategies and report back to the district what is and what is not working. Leaders should enthusiastically encourage this feedback, as it can increase the effectiveness of district initiatives.

What else can we do to make the playbook simpler or more useful?

The best tools are powerful and simple. The educators who are revising the playbook should be careful not to make it overly complicated, such as by adding strategies without removing others. Before any revisions are agreed to, the team needs to pause and consider whether they have made the playbook too complicated or if there is anything else they can do to make it simpler or more powerful.

What else should we do to improve the playbook?

This final question provides a last chance for the team to consider any additional ways in which the playbook can be improved. This discussion is also an opportunity for the facilitator to congratulate everyone on their hard work.

The Informal After-Implementation Review

Coaches don't need to wait until the formal AIR meetings to discuss what they are learning about the playbook. Indeed, they should use every chance they have to share their learning. Such sharing of knowledge can occur in informal conversations, through online documents, via email, through meeting apps like Zoom, and so forth. Whenever coaches get together, they should build in time to discuss the playbook.

To Sum Up

Instructional playbooks are organizational tools used by professional developers to identify high-impact teaching strategies and explain those strategies to teachers so the teachers and their students can meet powerful goals. Playbooks consist of three sections: a one-page table of contents that outlines the material included; one-pagers that summarize the research, purpose, and use of each strategy; and checklists designed for use by coaches to make it easier for teachers to implement teaching strategies effectively.

The instructional playbook is a living document, and as such it should be revised in formal meetings two to four times a year. The playbook should also be reviewed during any meetings of instructional coaches working from the same document.

Reflection Questions

1. Do you think you and your colleagues need to create an instructional playbook? Why or why not?
2. What strategies do you think should be included in a playbook?
3. When has the "curse of knowledge" made it difficult for you to explain a strategy?

4. Which elements of the one-pager do you think should be kept? What would you add to or remove from the one-pager?

5. When have you witnessed someone explaining a strategy with "false clarity"?

6. What is your initial reaction to the idea of a checklist?

7. Should you create a process to ensure that the instructional playbook is continuously improved? Why or why not?

Going Deeper

- Many of the ideas in this chapter are described in more detail in *The Instructional Playbook,* which Ann Hoffman, Michelle Harris, Sharon Thomas, and I published in 2020.

- Another major influence on this chapter is *The Checklist Manifesto* (2011), Atul Gawande's excellent book on why checklists are essential tools for improving any profession.

- I recommend several books that educators can refer to as they create their own instructional playbook in *High-Impact Instruction* (Knight, 2013), which is a kind of companion piece to *The Instructional Playbook,* mentioned above.

- Publications I've referred to as part of creating instructional playbooks include Jon Saphier, Mary Ann Haley-Speca, and Robert Gower's *The Skillful Teacher* (2017); Robert Marzano, Debra Pickering, and Jane Pollock's *Classroom Instruction That Works* (2001); and John Hattie's *Visible Learning for Teachers* (2009).

What's Next?

The next step is to actually create an instructional playbook. This might involve bringing together a team of educators to design a complete playbook, most likely working from the suggestions in our book on the topic. However, it could also start more informally, with coaches discussing what strategies should be in the playbook and then creating checklists for those strategies. The informal start might lead to the formation of a playbook development team, or the playbook might simply be developed over time during meetings.

How a coaching team arrives at the creation of a playbook isn't what matters; what matters is that coaches know the high-impact strategies they are sharing and that they have the tools necessary to describe those strategies. It also matters that the playbook is continuously improved by documenting what everyone is learning about teaching strategies. When coaches pay attention to what they are learning, the teachers they partner with learn more—and so do their students.

Where You Work

Learning Map for Chapter 7

System Support

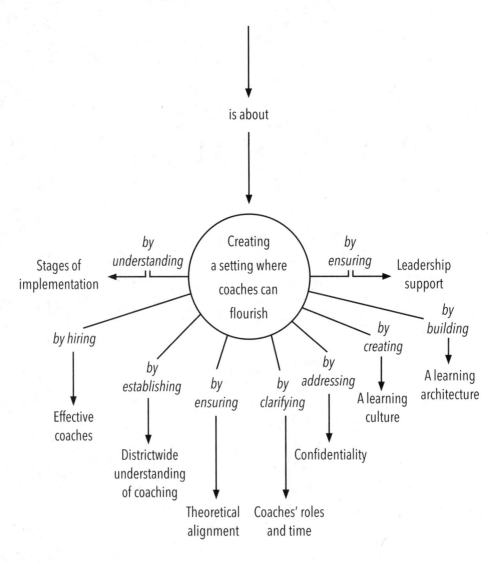

is about

Creating a setting where coaches can flourish

by understanding → Stages of implementation

by ensuring → Leadership support

by building → A learning architecture

by creating → A learning culture

by addressing → Confidentiality

by clarifying → Coaches' roles and time

by ensuring → Theoretical alignment

by establishing → Districtwide understanding of coaching

by hiring → Effective coaches

7 System Support

*We need to be working on all different parts of the system in
order to successfully change the whole system.*

—Peter Senge, *The Fifth Discipline*

Cameron Muir had "a lot of sleepless nights," he told us, after he suggested
coaching as a new approach to professional development in his school. Cameron, the associate principal for curriculum and instruction, had seen firsthand what coaching did for him when he was coached as a math teacher and
was convinced that coaching could have the same positive impact on teachers
and students at Glenbrook South. But Cameron's enthusiasm wasn't shared
by every other district leader. From the beginning, some leaders questioned
the costs and benefits of coaching.

Still, Cameron persisted. After his proposal was adopted, he had to
answer lots of questions and risk the disapproval of many colleagues who
openly doubted whether coaching would work.

Some of Cameron's anxiety likely stemmed from the fact that it took a
while before results started showing. But he never gave up. When one of the
school's coaches expressed disappointment that he'd only worked with a
small number of teachers, Cameron used a math analogy to remind the coach
of exponential growth. "We have small numbers now, but this model will ultimately grow dramatically," he said.

More than anything else, Cameron was intentional in the way he oversaw the coaching program. One of his first steps was to focus on one model
of coaching, which turned out to be the Impact Cycle. Then, to make sure he
fully understood it, he and the coaches from his school came to our ICG institute in Kansas. Soon afterward, he also set up a long-term partnership with
Northwestern University so that his coaches could attend the yearly institutes they offer in partnership with ICG.

Cameron learned a lot about instructional coaching and actively worked
to support the coaches in his school, but he made sure not to micromanage
his team. He was careful to hire excellent people, including Sharon Sheehan,
who served both as a coach and as a coaching supervisor. Together, Cameron

and Sharon worked to achieve a long-term vision for coaching at Glenbrook South.

Sharon recognized early on that she and her coaches would need training, so she asked our organization to provide coaching. Dr. Marti Elford from ICG met frequently with both Sharon and the other coaches at the school, as Sharon felt it was essential that they received training, too.

Sharon led the team to engage in other activities that increased their knowledge and skills, such as creating an instructional playbook (see Chapter 6). Many coaches went through the rigorous certification process that ICG offers for instructional coaches. And all coaches attended the institutes for new and advanced coaches offered by both Northwestern and ICG.

It took time, but they got results. In the 2018–19 school year, 233 of 240 teachers reported that they had worked with a coach at some point. Alison Gordon, who directs the Northwestern Coaching Institute and whose children attended Glenbrook South, told us about the changes she saw in the school:

> The thing that stands out about Glenbrook South is that there seems to be a shift of culture where teachers understand that for students to grow, teachers need to grow. The culture has shifted to a growth mindset where teachers are always learning and growing and working with people to perfect their craft and learn new things. Many people are clamoring to work with a coach. They want to get better.

In 2021, the decision makers at the second high school in Cameron's district decided that they wanted to have a coaching program similar to the one Cameron had developed.

The coaching program at Glenbrook South was successful because Cameron took a long view. He learned about coaching, hired people with the right skills, ensured that the coaches got the support they needed, and created a system in which the coaches could flourish. This, in my experience, is the only way to make coaching work. If we want our coaches to flourish, we need to create the conditions for success. Learning and change are too complicated and complex to happen by chance.

According to my count, there are at least nine interrelated issues that need to be addressed for coaches to succeed the way they do at Glenbrook South. Each of these issues is discussed in this chapter:

1. Understanding stages of implementation
2. Hiring effective coaches
3. Establishing districtwide understanding of coaching
4. Ensuring theoretical alignment
5. Clarifying roles and time
6. Addressing confidentiality
7. Creating a learning culture
8. Building a learning architecture
9. Ensuring leadership support

Understanding Stages of Implementation

Everyone wants results quickly because children's lives are significantly affected by the instruction they experience in school. But quick fixes are not real fixes. When we seriously consider how complex it is to learn and internalize an innovation, we start to see why quick fixes almost always fail.

To better understand the complexities of change, I've constructed a five-stage model of implementation based on the work of James Prochaska and colleagues (1994) and Gene Hall and Shirley Hord (2019). Prochaska and colleagues describe change as involving nonlinear movement through the following six stages:

1. Pre-contemplation
2. Contemplation
3. Preparation
4. Action
5. Maintenance
6. Termination

For their part, Hall and Hord propose eight "levels of use" in their concerns-based adoption model:

1. Non-use
2. Orientation

3. Preparation
4. Mechanical use
5. Routine use
6. Refinement
7. Integration
8. Renewal

By synthesizing both of these models with my own understanding of implementation developed through hundreds of interviews with teachers, coaches, and administrators over the past two decades, I have developed the five-stage implementation shown here.

Stages of Implementation

1. Non-use
2. Awareness
3. Mechanical
4. Routine
5. Proficient

Stage 1: Non-Use

During the non-use stage, people are not implementing an innovation because they are either unable or unwilling to do so. For one thing, they may not be able to implement innovations, such as the Identify questions described in Chapter 5, simply because they don't know about them, having missed the workshop or not read this book. Then again, people may be in the non-use stage because they either actively or passively resist the new learning. Active resisters make it clear that they choose not to implement whatever innovation is being proposed. Passive resisters quietly choose not to implement an innovation for reasons they keep to themselves.

Stage 2: Awareness

During the awareness stage, people know something about an innovation and are not resistant, but are also not implementing it. At this stage, they have a little knowledge but are unclear about how to put that new knowledge into practice. The longer they go without implementing the innovation, the less likely they are to ever do so. For example, coaches might attend a workshop on the Identify questions and be excited about using them, but as time passes without implementing them, they remember them less and less and eventually forget them altogether.

Stage 3: Mechanical

During the mechanical stage, people start to implement an innovation but often feel awkward about it because they have to remember a lot of new information in order to change their entrenched patterns of behavior. The mechanical stage can feel like walking through a field of deep, wet snow: messy, slow, uncomfortable, and tiring. A coach who is implementing the Identify questions, for example, may keep a list of questions nearby during coaching conversations, feel awkward asking the questions, or do more talking than listening during coaching.

Stage 4: Routine

During the routine stage of implementation, people start to become comfortable with aspects of the new strategy or skill they are learning. This can feel reassuring, especially after the struggles encountered during the mechanical stage. But feeling comfortable may tempt people to implement the innovation in a way that is easy to remember while leaving them hesitant to move beyond their comfortable, routine use. For example, coaches using the Identify questions may be tempted to ask the same questions in the same order every time they meet with teachers to set goals rather than adapting the questions to find the optimal prompts to encourage individual teachers as they reflect and plan.

In other words, a major risk of routine implementation is false clarity, which "occurs when change is interpreted in an oversimplified way; that is, the proposed change has more to it than people perceive or realize" (Fullan,

2001, p. 77). When we have false clarity, we are not implementing an innovation as effectively as we think we are, and that means we probably aren't having the impact that we desire. Effective, informed modification of an innovation is only possible during the proficient stage.

Stage 5: Proficient

When people arrive at the proficient stage, they have developed a deep understanding of the innovation they are learning and know how to modify it, if necessary, to increase its impact. Coaches who have reached the proficient stage in their questioning skills, for example, have developed a deep knowledge of coaching questions, have learned other powerful questions, are able to read their collaborating teacher's body language, and know to ask the right question at the right time to help the teacher reflect or plan. They can do this because they have learned, practiced, and modified questioning in many coaching conversations.

When people use an innovation proficiently, it can appear as if they are able to modify it without applying any effort at all. But what appears to be effortless is, in truth, the product of learning, practice, and experimentation over time. It takes a lot of work to look like you are implementing an innovation effortlessly.

Hiring Effective Coaches

Moving from one stage to the next can feel uncomfortable at first, like a trapeze artist who has to let go of one bar and hang in the air before grabbing the next. For this reason, coaches need sophisticated knowledge and skills to help teachers find success—which means those who are leading coaching programs need to hire the most qualified people possible. In fact, hiring the right coach may be the single most important part of ensuring coaching success.

Two important studies describe the characteristics of effective coaches. More than a decade ago, my colleagues and I at the University of Kansas, with the help of the State of Florida Department of Education, conducted a qualitative study using the naturalistic inquiry method (Guba & Lincoln, 1985) to identify the characteristics of effective coaches (Knight et al., 2010). Our findings showed that the most effective coaches

- Employ an array of interpersonal skills that enable them to develop collaborative, professional relationships with teachers.
- Effectively listen to the perspectives, opinions, and concerns of teachers.
- Are learners who have a lot of useful knowledge and skills.
- Love their work and are skilled at creating coaching opportunities while helping to build a cohesive school community.

The second study is Rebecca Frazier's comprehensive look at the characteristics of effective coaches in her book *The Joy of Coaching* (2021). Her quantitative study involved analyzing and summarizing 279 evaluative surveys of 43 coaches, 15 qualitative interviews, and growth results for 69 coaches. Frazier found that effective coaches are

- Collaborative;
- Caring;
- Competent;
- Authentic;
- Quality communicators;
- Inspirational;
- Flexible;
- Trustworthy;
- Well organized; and
- Effective at modeling practices.

Both studies show that coaches need to be emotionally intelligent or have what we commonly refer to as "soft skills." And soft skills are hard to learn. Leaders can teach coaches the teaching strategies that are included in an instructional playbook, but teaching them to be authentic, effective listeners who care is much more of a challenge. That is why it is so important to hire people who already are emotionally intelligent. To identify the best candidates, consider the suggestions below.

The Screening Interview

To ensure that you have time to pursue in-depth interviews, I suggest starting by conducting short interviews to eliminate candidates who are not qualified or appropriate for the position. These interviews should be no longer than 30 minutes and can take place online if that is most convenient for everyone. In their book *Who* (2008), Geoff Smart and Randy Street suggest these four screening interview questions:

1. What are your career goals?
2. What are you really good at professionally?
3. What are you not good at or not interested in doing professionally?
4. Who were your last five bosses, and how will they each rate your performance on a 1–10 scale when we talk to them? (p. 70)

According to Smart and Street, only 10 to 20 percent of people should make it through the first interview.

The Skills Interview

Interviewers will naturally want to gather information on what potential coaches know about teaching, curriculum, and coaching, but a coaching interview that focuses entirely on what the coach knows runs the risk of failing to identify the most emotionally intelligent candidate, potentially leading to the wrong hire.

I suggest that at least 50 percent of the skills interview focus on soft skills. Interviewers should ask questions that give them insight into how the candidate builds relationships, resolves conflict, and thinks flexibly. For example, during our interviews with the Pathways to Success project in Topeka, Kansas, we asked such questions as "What's a conflict you've had and how did you resolve it?" "What kind of people do you struggle to get along with?" "How would you go about getting to know people in your new school?" "What do you need to do to be a better communicator?" and "What is the last book you read that really changed you?" Of course, you will need to develop the best questions for your setting.

The Model Interview

After the screening and skills interviews, interviewers should have enough data to reduce the number of candidates significantly. Candidates who remain should then be asked to perform an additional task. When we contact candidates to let them know they have made it through the first stage of interviews, we explain that the next part of the interview will be to demonstrate a teaching strategy: they will need to come to our offices and pick up a short manual, then come back the next day to explain the strategies from the manual, which they've likely never seen before, to our team.

This task is incredibly revealing, showing us how quickly people learn new tasks, how committed they are to the job (some never come back for the model interview), how clearly they communicate, how effectively they handle stress, and many other soft skills. After we have seen all the model presentations, we usually know whom we want to hire.

Another option is to ask candidates to have a coaching conversation, and that might work best for you. However, we feel that our experiential learning activity shows us more about the character of the person and about whether the candidate will be able to go into a classroom and model practices.

The References Interview

A final suggestion is to carefully consider what you learn from the references a candidate provides. The first things you should determine are how well the reference knows the candidate and how long they worked together. Then, when talking with the references, pay careful attention to anything that suggests the candidate is less than ideal. Make sure you don't fall prey to confirmation bias because you really want to hire a candidate. Listen deeply to what people tell you.

One coaching leader I know once had a reference say, "Oh, she's doing so much better at getting along with everyone." That should have been a clue to the administrator, but she really wanted to hire the candidate. Two weeks after the hire, she started to wonder how she could move her out of the position.

Understand the Position Before You Hire for It

It's difficult to hire the right person for a position if you're not clear on what that position entails. For this reason, leaders need to clarify exactly what coaches are expected to do and not do. Additionally, leaders may want to create an instructional coaches' job scope like the one in Figure 7.1. As Smart and Street (2008) write, "You wouldn't think of having someone build you a house without an architect's blueprint in hand. Don't think of hiring people for your team without this blueprint by your side" (p. 19).

FIGURE 7.1

Instructional Coaches' Job Scope

Mission

To partner with teachers so that teachers move through coaching cycles that involve getting a clear picture of reality; setting PEERS goals; identifying, explaining, and modeling strategies; and partnering with teachers to make adaptations until goals are met.

Outcomes

- Within the first 60 days on the job, the instructional coach will be proficient in using the Impact Cycle (described in Chapters 2–5 of *The Impact Cycle* [Knight, 2018] and summarized by the checklist on p. 107 in *The Reflection Guide to the Impact Cycle*).
- Within the first 60 days, the instructional coach will be proficient in describing and modeling the teaching strategies included in the district's instructional playbook.
- Within the first 60 days, the instructional coach will be proficient in gathering and explaining the various types of engagement and achievement data described in *The Definitive Guide to Instructional Coaching*.
- By the end of the academic year, the instructional coach will have partnered with at least 40 teachers to set and meet PEERS goals.
- Each week, the instructional coach will watch at least one video of his or her coaching conversations and apply the after-implementation review questions ("What was supposed to happen?" "What really happened?" "What accounts for the difference?" "What will I do next time?") to identify areas for improvement.

Competencies

The instructional coach is

- *A learner:* open to change, seeking out new information, flexible and adaptive in implementation of materials, seeking out and internalizing feedback until proficient in strategies, and coachable.
- *An excellent communicator:* demonstrating outstanding listening and questioning skills and able to make positive emotional connections with others.
- *An encourager:* positive, affirmative, nonjudgmental, fully present in conversation, and respectful of teachers and all other educators and students.
- *Reliable:* organized and keen to provide scaffolding for others who are not highly organized, persistent, or ambitious to change.

The instructional coaches' job scope (or scorecard, as Smart and Street call it) "describes the mission for the position, the outcomes that must be accomplished, and competencies that fit with both the culture of the company and the role" (Smart & Street, 2008, p. 19). As instructional coach Kevin Heron told us after we sent the job scope out for review, "A document like this will help to get instructional coaches back to coaching first, other responsibilities second."

Establishing Districtwide Understanding of Coaching

Coaches are not the only people who need to understand what coaching is and is not. In settings where district leaders, teachers, and other educators don't understand coaching, coaches will struggle to succeed. Lack of such understanding may result in coaches being asked to act in ways that are inconsistent with coaching best practices, or they may encounter educators who are hesitant to work with them because they don't actually know what coaches do. To prevent such situations, district leaders should offer professional development and learning so that everyone understands what coaching is, what coaches do, and how they can support coaches.

Leaders can encourage widespread knowledge about coaching through a combination of professional development workshops and follow-up small-group and one-to-one professional learning support. Four topics are especially important:

1. The way of being that underlies the coaching program, which we describe as the partnership approach.
2. The key elements of the coaching process, which for us is the Impact Cycle.
3. Strategic knowledge, which includes the instructional playbook and how data are gathered.
4. The coaching habits and skills that stand at the heart of better conversations: listening, questioning, demonstrating empathy, fostering trust, and engaging in dialogue.

One way to guide discussion about what coaching is and isn't is to share and discuss a T-chart like the one in Figure 7.2. The facilitator of the conversation should have a deep and nuanced understanding of what each item on the list is and why it is important.

FIGURE 7.2	
Coaching T-Chart	
Coaching Is...	Coaching Is Not...
A partnership relationship	A top-down relationship
Guided by emotionally compelling goals chosen by the person implementing them	Guided by goals that are chosen for people by people outside the teacher's classroom
Authentic learning	Going through the motions
Responsible accountability	Irresponsible accountability
Commitment	Compliance
A process that positively improves student learning and engagement	A process that targets teaching practices
Nonevaluative	Evaluative
Affirming	Moralistically judgmental

Ensuring Theoretical Alignment

The quickest way forward in school is to conduct professional development that honors each teacher's professionalism, which for us entails a grounding in the Partnership Principles of equality, choice, voice, dialogue, reflection, praxis, and reciprocity (see p. 6). For this reason, I suggest that everyone in a district learn and apply the Partnership Principles in their interactions with others. People should be encouraged to read Chapter 2 of this book to see the research behind this approach and prompted to take their knowledge deeper by creating concept diagrams or similar graphic organizers for each principle and by exploring cases that clarify the practical implications of the partnership approach.

Of course, when we share the Partnership Principles, we must work from them. This means that we encourage people to say what is on their minds (voice), that we encourage them to adapt the principles to their unique situations (choice), that we encourage meaningful exploratory conversation about the implications of the principles (dialogue), and that we collectively and individually explore how the principles apply to real-life situations (praxis).

Although the partnership approach is nominally embraced by most people, it can be challenging to accept because it represents a different way of understanding how professional development occurs. Peter Senge described this organizational challenge in *The Fifth Discipline* (1990):

> Many of the best ideas never get put into practice. Brilliant strategies fail to get translated into action.... We are coming increasingly to believe that this... stems, not from weak intentions, wavering will, or even nonsystemic understanding, but from mental models. More specifically, new insights fail to get put into practice because they conflict with deeply held internal images of how the world works, images that limit us to familiar ways of thinking and acting. (p. 174)

Leaders can help people break out of their limiting mental models by acknowledging that the model exists, by fostering deep understanding of the Partnership Principles, and by experimenting with the principles to see what impact they have on relationships as well as on teacher and student learning. If people take the risk to learn and try out the principles, they will see results, and when they see results, they will be more interested in changing.

The Partnership Principles can also be challenging because they appear to ask people to give up power, and most people don't want to do that. However, the power that comes from a top-down model of change is given to leaders only because of their position, and the power that comes from partnerships is much more valuable because it comes from others' authentic commitment.

Clarifying Coaches' Roles and Time

When we ask coaches to describe the roadblocks they experience in their work, they almost always bring up two issues: (1) coaches don't have enough time to complete coaching cycles, and (2) most people, including the coaches themselves, aren't clear on what instructional coaches are supposed to do. Fortunately, coaches and administrators can go a long way toward removing these roadblocks by using a form like the one in Figure 7.3 to clarify what coaches should do and what percentage of their time they should spend on each task.

FIGURE 7.3		
Instructional Coaches' Task Chart		
Task	**Yes/No**	**Time %**
The Impact Cycle		
Leading workshops		
Implementation support		
Mentoring		
Leading professional learning communities and teams		
Conducting walkthroughs		
Assessments (including giving tests, analyzing data, reporting, etc.)		
Curriculum		
Professional knowledge building		
Relationship building		
Monitoring and learning from time spent		
Substitute teaching		
Cafeteria duty		
Bus duty		

The Impact Cycle

We have found that, on average, it takes about six contact hours for coaches to move through the Impact Cycle. The length of cycles can vary from two to three weeks to a whole semester (or more), so planning should be flexible enough to accommodate shorter or longer cycles.

When full-time instructional coaches spend all their time on the Impact Cycle, they are generally able to work with 10 teachers at a time. Additional tasks reduce the time coaches are able to spend on the Impact Cycle, which, in turn, reduces the number of teachers with whom a coach can partner and, consequently, the coach's impact.

Leading Workshops

There are many advantages to coaches leading workshops even though it takes time away from one-to-one coaching. First, the work that goes into preparing for workshops deepens coaches' knowledge. Second, coaches can prove their credibility by presenting effectively. Third, a workshop is an effective way to enroll people in coaching, and every workshop should include a sign-up form for that purpose.

But workshops do not replace coaching. While they provide an overview of content, they rarely lead to implementation, in part because we quickly forget a lot of what we learn during a workshop. Deep implementation requires learning in action and follow-up, which we refer to as *implementation support*.

Implementation Support

When coaches provide implementation support, they use the tools of coaching to help teachers master new teaching strategies. Working from the Partnership Principles, they collaborate with teachers to set goals related to high-quality implementation rather than ones that are student-focused. They describe strategies using checklists, ensure teachers watch the strategy being implemented, use video to record lessons so teachers can see and reflect on how they teach a strategy, and partner with teachers to make adjustments when necessary.

A major challenge with implementation support is that teachers who focus on strategies rather than student-focused goals may be less motivated and less likely to sustain implementation, because focusing on student learning and well-being is usually more motivating than focusing on what we do. However, if leaders in a district adopt particular approaches to math, science, language arts, or some other subject, implementation support is essential.

For this reason, in some districts, coaches spend most of their time leading workshops and providing implementation support.

Mentoring

I define *mentoring* as a long- or short-term relationship in which an experienced person shares particular knowledge with a less experienced person. Mentoring is most effective when the coach responds to a need expressed by the collaborating teacher. For example, a teacher who wants to learn how to help students create a word map using special software probably doesn't want her coach to ask, "When have you been successful learning software in the past?" Instead, she just wants to know how to do it.

During long-term mentoring, experienced educators share their expertise with younger educators in one-to-one conversations. For a new teacher, the advice of an experienced mentor on the day-to-day work of teaching can be helpful and reassuring.

By contrast, short-term mentoring occurs when people share their expertise about a particular technology, idea, or strategy. During the COVID-19 pandemic, for example, when many educators needed to master numerous technology tools quickly, instructional coaches had to provide a lot of quick support just to ensure their teachers were able to implement the various forms of technology they needed to use.

Leading Professional Learning Communities and Teams

Some coaches are asked to lead professional learning communities (PLCs). This will consume a lot of time that could be spent moving teachers through the Impact Cycle. Such a commitment may be worthwhile when PLCs collaborate around an emotionally compelling PEERS goal that everyone sees as a powerful response to student needs. However, if members of a team are trying to meet a goal that they don't really care about, they are usually not very motivated. For that reason, I suggest that coaching start out one-to-one and only move to teams when the coach is certain that the members of the team are deeply committed to a shared goal.

In some situations, coaches are asked to lead PLCs because school administrators want to ensure that teachers' collaborative meeting time is used productively. But if PLCs are not working, the solution is not to have coaches oversee the teachers; it's to provide enough time and professional development for the PLCs to function effectively. A Band-Aid on a problem is always inferior to a real solution, especially when it keeps coaches from partnering with teachers.

Conducting Walkthroughs

Many administrators use walkthroughs to learn what is happening in each teacher's classroom and to give teachers quick evaluative feedback. However, I do not recommend that coaches conduct walkthroughs for a few reasons.

First, when coaches conduct walkthroughs, no matter how their role is described, they will be perceived as administrators, and people often hesitate to be candid with those who evaluate them. Additionally, since coaches usually have not been trained to be administrators, there is a good chance that they don't have the necessary qualifications to be evaluating teachers.

Second, the top-down feedback that results from walkthroughs is often ignored (Buckingham & Goodall, 2019). Feedback that has the best chance of leading to change is self-generated: a teacher watches a video of her lesson, perhaps with an observation tool in hand, and then discusses the lesson with the coach. As a friend of mine likes to say, "Glow and grow has got to go!"

In some settings, coaches are asked to do walkthroughs because principals can't or won't do them. But again, this is a Band-Aid on a larger problem that needs to be solved at a more fundamental level.

Assessments

Instructional coaches may be assigned many responsibilities related to assessing students, such as circulating or giving tests, gathering data, analyzing data, and writing reports. None of these are coaching tasks, but someone needs to do them. Some districts hire assessment coordinators to oversee everything related to assessment, which frees up coaches to actually coach. However, in cases where coaches are involved in assessment, it is important that administrators and coaches accurately consider how much time assessment may take and that leaders adjust their expectations for coaching based on the time coaches actually are able to apply to coaching.

Curriculum

In some districts, coaches perform many tasks related to curriculum. Often, coaches create curriculum and then help individual teachers or teams of teachers to implement it. In my experience, curriculum development is most productive when teachers are involved and when the final product includes high-impact teaching practices like guiding questions, learning maps, and formative assessment. (In my book *Unmistakable Impact* [Knight, 2011], I describe intensive learning teams that involve all instructors in the creation of curriculum.)

It must be noted that when coaches play a major role in the development and dissemination of curriculum, they have much less time for guiding teachers through the coaching cycles. Leaders need to think carefully about what coaches need to do to have the most positive impact on students' lives.

Professional Knowledge Building

Anyone who becomes an instructional coach encounters a steep learning curve, since coaching involves completely new knowledge and skills. Specifically, new coaches need to learn and apply a way of being as outlined in the Partnership Principles, a process such as the Impact Cycle, teaching strategies (which they will likely need to organize into an instructional playbook), and data gathering, as well as coaching and communication skills such as listening, asking powerful questions, explaining strategies dialogically, and so forth. Coaches won't learn all of this by chance; they need time to gather, practice, and improve their knowledge and skills.

Coaches can expand their knowledge by reading books about instruction and coaching, attending workshops, meeting with their peers, watching video of their coaching practices, and reflecting on what's working and what isn't working. Essentially, coaches need to have time to address all of the Success Factors described in this book. Ensuring coaches have time to learn is one of the most important investments coaching leaders can make.

Relationship Building

Coaches engage in informal conversations all the time, but the most meaningful professional conversations don't start until after they engage with teachers in a coaching cycle. So when I hear coaches say, "I'm spending my first semester just building relationships," I worry that they may never start coaching.

Like all important learning, figuring out the Impact Cycle pushes new coaches out of their comfort zone. Not surprisingly, some of them prefer to remain comfortably engaged in informal interactions. But real growth happens when coaches and teachers move through the Impact Cycle, and a coach who is unwilling to engage in that cycle likely won't have any real impact.

Monitoring and Learning from Time Spent

Coaches can learn a lot by monitoring their time and making adjustments to ensure they are being as productive as possible. The easiest way to do this is to complete a daily time log and transfer the time recorded to a spreadsheet application such as Excel or Numbers at the end of the day or week. The spreadsheet will reveal how coaches actually spent their time.

At regular intervals, coaches and principals should review this log to ensure that the principal doesn't assign the coach too many tasks that are not focused on coaching. A supportive principal will fight to ensure that coaches have the time they need to actually coach.

Other Duties as Assigned

Coaches may be asked to perform any of the following other duties within a district.

Substitute teaching

Coaches solve an urgent problem when they substitute teach. However, doing this also means they have to cancel and reschedule all their appointments for the day. In many cases, this means that they will have to postpone meeting with teachers until the next week or later, which will decrease the sense of urgency surrounding the collaborative work they're engaging in. One day of substitute teaching disrupts 20 percent of a coach's coaching partnerships for the week. That's a significant negative impact on coaching.

Of course, there are crisis situations in which no one is available to teach a class. We suggest coaches fill in during those emergencies at the same rate the principal and other administrators do.

Cafeteria and bus duty

The advantage of coaches doing bus and cafeteria duty is that they will be perceived by others in the school as equal partners, willing to roll up their sleeves and do the tasks that others do. The downside is that teachers are often free when bus and cafeteria duty happen and, therefore, available to meet with their coach. Additionally, time spent in the cafeteria is time coaches don't spend on coaching, and it is through coaching that they have the greatest impact on student engagement and achievement. For these reasons, we suggest coaches not engage in bus or cafeteria duty but, rather, use that time to partner with teachers.

Addressing Confidentiality

Most authors and researchers describe coaching as a confidential or at least somewhat confidential relationship, and for good reason. Asking them to share evaluative information about teachers with principals puts coaches into a quasi-administrative position and upsets the equality inherent in most coaching conversations. As mentioned previously in this book, status is at play in most professional conversations, and when people do not feel they are getting the status they deserve, they are less likely to engage in learning (Schein, 2009).

Does this mean, then, that coaching should always be confidential? When I spoke with a well-respected educational leader about this, he said that he didn't think so. From his perspective, schools need to be psychologically safe settings where everyone is open and transparent about the practices in their classroom. In his opinion, any secrecy in a school inhibits professional learning, and leaders need to work to create settings where people feel comfortable sharing with everyone what they are experiencing in their classroom.

I appreciate this perspective, and when you are in a setting that is psychologically safe, I think it is absolutely correct. A school where everyone feels comfortable opening their doors to everyone else and sharing what they are doing is a school where educators are learning. But that school needs to have a coaching culture in place, so I suggest leaders move cautiously before deciding to turn away from confidential coaching. Administrators should, of course, be given the time to see practices in each teacher's classroom without the coach having to share evaluative information.

What matters most is that administrators, coaches, and teachers are all clear on the policy for confidentiality and that the policy is honored. If a teacher thinks coaching is confidential and then discovers that it is not, that teacher will lose trust, and real learning rarely occurs when teachers don't trust their coaches.

Creating a Learning Culture

Culture can make or break a coaching program. In schools with healthy, learning cultures, teachers feel safe, supported, and excited about the opportunity to collaborate and learn with their peers. In schools with unhealthy, stuck cultures, teachers feel alone, judged, and demoralized. People usually feel the power of culture the moment they enter a school they've never visited before.

According to Susan Rosenholtz (1989), teacher behavior is usually not the result of individual choices or "good" or "bad" behavior. Rather, she writes, "teachers... shape their beliefs and actions largely in conformance with the structures, policies and traditions of the workaday world around them" (pp. 2–3). Rosenholtz adapts Rosabeth Moss Kanter's distinction between "stuck" and "moving" cultures to distinguish between unhealthy and healthy learning cultures:

> The stuck feel no sense of progress, growth or development and so tend to lower their aspirations and appear less motivated to achieve. They shy away from risks in the workplace and proceed in cautious, conservative ways. The moving, by contrast, tend to recognize and use more of their skills and aim still higher. Their sense of progress and future gain encourages them to look forward, to take risks, and to grow. (p. 149)

Harvard researcher Amy Edmondson summarizes research that expands our understanding of culture in her book *The Fearless Organization* (2019). The best learning environments, Edmondson writes, are those in which people feel psychologically safe, which she defines as "the experience of feeling able to speak up with relevant ideas, questions, or concerns. Psychological safety is present when colleagues trust and respect each other and feel able—even obligated—to be candid" (p. 8). Psychological safety is essential because people who are afraid usually aren't learning. Coaching, therefore, is much more likely to flourish in schools with psychologically safe cultures.

These ideas are easy to type on a computer, but not so easy to carry out in an organization. However, every committed educator in a school can work to create such a safe environment. Teachers can do this by refraining from moralistically judging others or by inviting others into their classroom to learn. Coaches can do this by admitting their imperfections and by approaching colleagues with humility.

But it's the principal who has the greatest potential to have an impact on creating a psychologically safe environment, and Edmondson has some suggestions. Leaders, she writes, need to do all they can to eliminate fear in the environment. This means, especially, that they need to develop the capacity to hear others' stresses and criticisms without taking them personally. Leaders need to reward others for taking risks rather than criticizing them for failing. They need to be curious and admit that they don't know everything. And they need to model learning by being learners themselves—and, especially, by learning from other educators in the school. For their part, others in the school can help leaders by forgiving them when they reveal their own imperfections.

Building a Learning Architecture

Our nervous system is like wiring for our body, sending information to and from the brain, spinal column, nerves, and more. We simply wouldn't be able to function without a nervous system.

Effective organizations should also have a nervous system—what I call their *learning architecture*. If a district chooses to put instructional coaches in place to support professional learning—and I hope this book is making the case that that's a very good idea!—learning architecture needs to be designed and implemented so that all individuals in the system are learning what they need to learn. This wiring for learning isn't just about ensuring everyone knows what they need to know; it is also a way of ensuring that the learning being discovered by everyone in the system—teachers, coaches, champions (see below), directors—is shared quickly with everyone. If the architecture is well designed and functioning well, then every time a teacher discovers a real insight about the teaching of a strategy, everyone in the district should hear about it in a matter of days.

Supporting Coaches' Learning

Coaching is essential for professional learning, but what about coaches? Don't they also need coaches? Of course they do: coaches need someone who will support their learning in the same way that coaches support teachers. We refer to these people as *coaching champions*.

Coaching champions are experts at the four dimensions of instructional coaching (way of being, coaching process, coaching and communication habits and skills, and strategic knowledge). Coaching champions help coaches adapt what they're doing until they are successfully helping teachers set and meet powerful goals.

You can probably guess where this is going. Does every champion need a coach? Yes, and that person is the one who directs the coaching program. At first, at least, the director may also need expert support—for example, from a consultant or an organization outside the district. Does this mean that everyone needs a coach? Yes. As coaching director Keysha McIntyre told us in an interview, "Every coach, no matter how great, needs a coach."

Gathering and Sharing Knowledge

One important part of learning architecture is that it maps out and ensures that learning takes place across an entire system. The learning isn't unidirectional, flowing down from the central office to coaches, teachers, and students. Learning should also flow back from students and teachers to the directors in the system. Indeed, much of the most important learning about strategies occurs when teachers try out a strategy and their learning flows back through the system.

For this to happen, learning has to take place vertically, in coaching conversations, and horizontally, in team meetings. Teachers need to be supported by coaches, but teachers also need to meet in PLCs. In addition, coaches, champions, and directors need to meet in instructional coaching professional learning communities (ICPLCs) so coaches can learn new ideas, practice coaching moves with others, review video of coaching and teaching, and share what they are learning. When left to chance, some learning may happen, but much more will occur when learning communities are created to promote important professional learning.

Coaches, champions, and the coaching director should meet at least twice a month. If a coaching program is just starting, meetings should probably occur weekly. In very large districts, ICPLCs may need to be divided into smaller groups so that everyone has an opportunity to share knowledge during meetings. ICPLCs can provide opportunities for coaches to

- Share what they are learning from students, teachers, and their own experiences;
- Review the instructional playbook;
- Practice coaching skills;
- Learn collectively in many other ways; and, perhaps most important,
- Support people doing the same job as them.

The coaching director, in partnership with the district superintendent, should create a similar professional learning community for central office staff, including the superintendent, assistant superintendent, directors, principals, and so forth. Such meetings ensure that everyone in the district understands how instructional coaching should be implemented, provide an opportunity for the coaching director to share information about the impact of coaching, and offer a chance for participants to ask questions about coaching as well as share their ideas, positive stories and results, and concerns. Finally, the meetings provide a venue for the coaching director to share what coaches are learning from teachers. Leaders need to hear when an innovation is succeeding and when teachers are finding that an innovation or a program isn't working.

Some may consider learning architecture to be overkill, and district decision makers facing tough budget constraints may be tempted not to fund it. There is a cost to hiring coaching champions and structuring time for the various meetings described here, but coaching that is poorly implemented is a much worse use of funds. Well-designed learning architecture provides the support coaches need to improve and succeed and offers a way for learning to be efficiently shared across a system. Schools should be learning organizations, and a learning architecture such as the one depicted in Figure 7.4 helps make that happen.

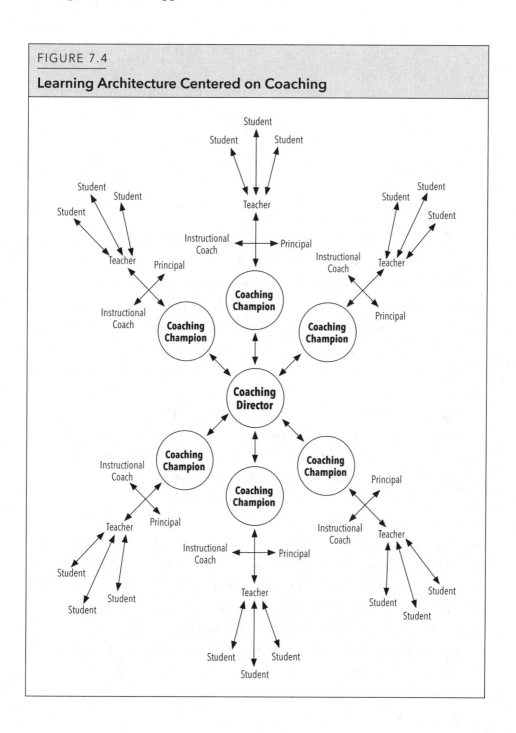

FIGURE 7.4

Learning Architecture Centered on Coaching

Ensuring Leadership Support

Coaches are much more likely to flourish when the principal in their school believes in coaching, is intentional about supporting them, and communicates the belief that coaching is very important. Most people want to do what the person they report to wants them to do, and if the principal communicates a belief in coaching, teachers will be much more likely to engage in productive coaching conversations. (The opposite, of course, is also true.)

Like all leaders, principals are more successful when they use effective leadership strategies. As I mention elsewhere in this book, the extensive literature on leadership has found that effective leaders are emotionally intelligent and excellent listeners who genuinely care about their employees and consequently build positive relationships. Effective leaders are motivated more by purpose than personal ego; somewhat paradoxically, they combine ambition for change with humility toward their colleagues.

Principals should implement the leadership strategies described in Chapter 3 both to lead themselves and to lead others. They can lead themselves by clarifying their purpose, managing their time effectively, developing good habits, and practicing self-care. They can lead others by balancing ambition with humility, being Multipliers, fostering alignment, and making good decisions.

Principals can support coaches by meeting with them to confirm the coach's responsibilities and the percentage of time to be spent on each assigned task, then to honor those arrangements. If a principal confirms that the coach knows what she is to do and ensures that she has the time to do those tasks, that is a huge step forward for coaching.

Everyone in school should be learning, and that starts with the principal. Principals demonstrate their learning by talking about the books they are reading, video-recording the meetings they lead and learning from those recordings, and embracing feedback that they receive from others. One way to walk the talk as learners is, as Malcolm Gladwell says (quoted in Holdengräber, 2014), to change your mind at least once a day.

Another great way for principals to walk the talk is to agree to be coached. Coaches might be employees within the district or external consultants. For example, ICG provides professional development in the GROWTH coaching model (see below) so that administrators can provide peer coaching. John Campbell, who first described GROWTH coaching with Christian van Nieuwerburgh in their book *The Leader's Guide to Coaching in Schools* (2018), coached me using GROWTH coaching in 2019. Thanks to my conversations with John, I became much more aware of the need to lead myself by developing healthier life habits, which I continue to do today.

Another model for administrator coaching is offered by professional development expert and former principal Bill Sommers, who has adapted Marshall Goldsmith's stakeholder coaching model (Goldsmith & Silvester, 2007) for use in schools (Hord, Roussin, & Sommers, 2000). During stakeholder coaching, the coach interviews several important people in the principal's life, asking them to identify what the principal is doing well and what the principal needs to change, and then helps the principal work to improve in one area. (When Bill coached me, he refused to be paid until I actually changed, which made the entire coaching experience extra-interesting.)

Finally, administrators can demonstrate their commitment to coaching by coaching others. Most principals won't have the time to move through more than one or two Impact Cycles, but they can use a facilitative approach to coaching like the previously mentioned GROWTH model developed by Campbell and van Nieuwerburgh (2018). Using this model, coaches partner with others to clarify goals, identify resources that exist in reality, generate options, identify what the collaborating person will do, pin down tactics, and plan how to make new behavior a habit (see below).

Goals: What do you need to achieve?
Reality: What is happening now?
Options: What could you do?
Will: What will you do?
Tactics: How and when will you do it?
Habits: How will you sustain your success?

Just like instructional coaches, principals need to learn how to do facilitative coaching, and they need to move through the stages of implementation described at the start of this chapter until they become proficient at it. When they become proficient, there is a good chance that they will be better communicators, better listeners, better leaders, and better supports for teachers. They will also be more effective at supporting coaches.

To Sum Up

Coaches who learn and implement the first six Success Factors described in this book will be well prepared to succeed. However, their success will be greatly limited if the seventh Success Factor, system support, is ignored. The most successful coaches work in settings where professional development is designed to help all professionals move through the stages of implementation to proficiency. This means that great care is taken to hire the best candidates for coaching positions.

Additionally, district leaders in such settings provide professional development to ensure that everyone involved in student learning understands the seven Success Factors of coaching and, in particular, that there is a shared understanding of the principles behind coaching, what coaches do and how they should spend their time, and the policy for confidentiality. District leaders need to be intentional about creating a psychologically safe learning culture and to show support for coaching, and they should design a learning architecture so that learning moves through the organization quickly and efficiently.

Reflection Questions

1. Does the professional development in your organization provide enough support for educators to become proficient in the practices they learn?
2. Does the organization have procedures in place to ensure that outstanding professionals are hired to be coaches?
3. Does everyone in the organization understand what instructional coaching is and what coaches do?

4. Do coaches have time to do what is expected of them? If not, what needs to change so that they do have the time?

5. Do people across the district agree on a set of principles, such as the Partnership Principles, that should guide coaching?

6. Do leaders support coaches?

7. Has the organization put in place a learning architecture to ensure that learning flows through the system efficiently?

Going Deeper

- One of the books I have found to be most useful for describing how to support coaches is actually not about coaches: *Cultures Built to Last* (2013) by Michael Fullan and Rick DuFour.
- *Coaching Matters* (2nd ed.; 2020) by Chris Bryan, Heather Clifton, and Joellen Killion discusses topics such as the hiring and placing of coaches, principal-coach relationships, coach champions, and the roles of coaches.
- *Agents of Change* (2013) by Antonia Cameron and Lucy West provides suggestions on the coach's role, principal support, and designing and refining coaching initiatives.
- Rebecca Frazier's *The Joy of Coaching* (2021) is a comprehensive guide to the characteristics of effective coaches.

What's Next?

Coaching has tremendous potential to have a powerfully positive impact on students' learning and well-being. But coaching likely won't succeed if the system doesn't support coaches. The nine areas discussed in this chapter are all crucial, and district leaders should review the suggestions and create a strategic plan that addresses each area. Some of the recommendations are quite simple, such as creating a policy on confidentiality, but others, like building a learning architecture, require more strategic planning. The good news, though, is that when district leaders take the time to carefully plan how to hire the best coaches and support them effectively, great things will happen for students.

Conclusion:
Coaching and a Well-Lived Life

I can think of few career choices better than being an instructional coach. Coaches partner with people to support them as they change their lives for the better, and at the same time, that work changes coaches' own lives for the better. Given what coaches do and what makes up a well-lived life, it is clear that almost everything a coach does touches some important part of a meaningful life.

A well-lived life involves learning, and learning is the primary work of coaching. As Peter Senge (1990) has written in perhaps my all-time favorite quote, "Through learning we re-create ourselves... [and]... we become able to do something we never were able to do. Through learning we reperceive the world and our relationship to it. Through learning we extend our capacity to create, to be part of the generative process of life.... There is within each of us a deep hunger for this type of learning" (p. 14). Coaches tap into this "deep hunger" for learning by partnering with teachers to create the conditions for better learning in classrooms, and through their partnerships with educators, coaches invite educators to become better learners. In the process, coaches are also constantly learning themselves—about people, students, strategies, and better ways of communicating.

A well-lived life is creative, and all effective coaches are creative. Like an artist mixing paint to find the perfect color for a work of art or a master chef mixing the ingredients to create a delicious dish, coaches creatively partner with educators to invent, adapt, and create new ways to reach the minds and hearts of more children. In all stages of the Impact Cycle, but especially during the Improve stage, coaches, in partnership with teachers, create new ways of teaching and learning so that students get the most out of every lesson.

A well-lived life is full of hope, and coaches build hope. As Shane Lopez and psychologist Rick Snyder have stated, and as I have explained in this book, hope involves three main elements: a positive future, pathways to that future, and agency (i.e., a belief that we have what it takes to follow the pathways to our positive future). Coaches foster hope by helping teachers identify a preferred future by clarifying goals, determine the pathways leading to that future by selecting strategies teachers can use to meet goals, and exert agency by gathering data showing that progress is being made.

A well-lived life involves rich relationships, and coaching is all about relationships. Coaches partner with educators so that educators can have better conversations with students and peers, and, in turn, coaches engage in deep and important conversations with those they coach. Such conversations help coaches have better conversations in their personal and professional lives. Indeed, many coaches report that their relationships improved when their coaching skills improved.

A well-lived life, finally, is a meaningful, purposeful life that makes the world a better place. And this is where coaching may be most important. Coaches partner with teachers to help them remind themselves of their purpose. As such, coaching invites teachers to move closer to a life where what they believe on the inside aligns with what they do on the outside. But most important, perhaps, coaches partner with teachers so they can have an unmistakably positive impact on children's lives. And when a coach helps a teacher make one positive change, that change can have an impact on every student that teacher ever teaches.

Learning, creativity, hope, relationships, purpose, and impact—what other job touches on so many of the most important aspects of a life well lived? Coaching isn't easy. It is challenging, and sometimes frustrating, because it involves infinitely complex work with other human beings. However, when their work is grounded in the seven Success Factors described in this book, coaches will help students, educators, and themselves live better lives.

References

Abrams, S. (2018, November). *3 questions to ask yourself about everything you do* [Video]. TED. Retrieved from www.youtube.com/watch?v=3zJHwOwirjA

Aguilar, E. (2013). *The art of coaching: Effective strategies for school transformation.* San Francisco: Jossey-Bass.

Ainsworth, L. (2015). *"Unwrapping" the Common Core: A practical process to manage rigorous standards.* Englewood, CO: Lead and Learn Press.

Ainsworth, L., & Viegut, D. (2014). *Common formative assessments 2.0: How teacher teams intentionally align standards, instruction, and assessment.* Thousand Oaks, CA: Corwin.

Allen, D. (2015). *Getting things done: The art of stress-free productivity.* New York: Penguin.

Allen, D. W., Cooper, J. M., & Fortune, J. C. (1967). The Stanford summer micro-teaching clinic, 1965. *Journal of Teaching Education, 18*(4), 389–393.

Amabile, T., Conti, R., Coon, H., Lazenby, J., & Herron, M. (1996). Assessing the work environment for creativity. *Academy of Management Journal, 39*(5), 1154–1184.

Amabile, T., & Kramer, S. (2011). *The progress principle: Using small wins to ignite joy, engagement, and creativity at work.* Boston: Harvard Business Review Press.

Anderson, L. W., & Krathwohl, D. R. (2001). *A taxonomy for learning, teaching, and assessing: A revision of Bloom's taxonomy of educational objectives* (Abridged; 1st ed.). New York: Pearson.

Angelou, M. (2018, August 12). *Do the best you can until you know better. Then when you know better, do better.* [Tweet]. Twitter. Retrieved from https://twitter.com/drmayaangelou/status/1028663286512930817

Arendt, H. (1958). *The human condition* (2nd ed.). Chicago: University of Chicago Press.

Aristotle. (1961). *Aristotle's poetics.* New York: Hill & Wang.

Baker, G. C. (2014). *Hot fudge sundae in a white paper cup: A spirited Black woman in a white world.* Ann Arbor, MI: University of Michigan Press.

Barkley, S. G. (2009). *Questions for life: Powerful strategies to guide critical thinking.* New York: Worthy Shorts.

Barkley, S. G. (2011). *Instructional coaching with the end in mind.* New York: Worthy Shorts.

Bate, W. J. (1963). *John Keats.* Cambridge, MA: Harvard University Press.

Berger, W. (2014). *A more beautiful question: The power of inquiry to spark breakthrough ideas.* New York: Bloomsbury.

Bernstein, R. J. (1983). *Beyond objectivism and relativism.* Philadelphia: University of Pennsylvania Press.

Berry, B., Smylie, M., & Fuller. E. (2008). *Understanding teacher working conditions: A review and look to the future.* Chapel Hill, NC: Center for Teaching Quality.

Bezos, J. (2016). *2016 letter to shareholders.* Retrieved from www.aboutamazon.com/company-news/2016-letter-to-shareholders

Birsel, A. (2015). *Design the life you love: A step-by-step guide to building a meaningful future.* Berkeley, CA: Ten Speed Press.

Block, P. (1993). *Stewardship: Choosing service over self-interest.* Oakland, CA: Berrett-Koehler.

Bohm, D. (1996). *On dialogue.* London: Routledge Taylor and Francis.

Boudet, K. P., City, E., & Murnane, R. (2005). *Data wise: A step-by-step guide to using assessment results to improve teaching and learning.* Cambridge, MA: Harvard Education Press.

Brennan-Nelson, D. (2005). *Someday is not a day of the week.* Ann Arbor, MI: Sleeping Bear Press.

Brock, A., & Hundley, H. (2016). *The growth mindset coach: A teacher's month-by-month handbook for empowering students to achieve.* New York: Simon & Schuster.

Brookhart, S. M. (2013). *How to create and use rubrics for formative assessment and grading.* Alexandria, VA: ASCD.

Brown, B. (2018). *Dare to lead: Brave work. Tough conversations. Whole hearts.* New York: Random House.

Bryan, C., Clifton, H., & Killion, J. (2020). *Coaching matters* (2nd ed.). Logan, UT: Jenson Books.

Buckingham, M., & Coffman, C. (1999). *First, break all the rules: What the world's greatest managers do differently.* New York: Simon & Schuster.

Buckingham, M., & Goodall, A. (2019, March–April). The feedback fallacy. *Harvard Business Review.* Retrieved from https://hbr.org/2019/03/the-feedback-fallacy

Bulgren, J., Schumaker, J., & Deshler, D. (1993). *The concept mastery routine.* Lawrence, KS: Edge Enterprises.

Bungay Stanier, M. (2016). *The coaching habit: Say less, ask more & change the way you lead forever.* Toronto, Canada: Box of Crayons Press.

Bungay Stanier, M. (2020). *The advice trap: Be humble, stay curious & change the way you lead forever.* Vancouver, Canada: Page Two Books.

Burgess, A. (1986). *A clockwork orange.* New York: Norton.

Camerer, C., Loewenstein, G., & Weber, M. (1989). The curse of knowledge in economic settings: An experimental analysis. *Journal of Political Economy, 97*(5), 1232–1254.

Cameron, A., & West, L. (2013). *Agents of change: How content coaching transforms teaching and learning.* Portsmouth, NH: Heinemann.

Campbell, J., & van Nieuwerburgh, C. (2018). *The leader's guide to coaching in schools: Creating conditions for effective learning.* Thousand Oaks, CA: Corwin.

Chappuis, J., & Stiggins, R. (2017). *Introduction to student-involved assessment for learning* (7th ed.). New York: Pearson.

Clear, J. (2018). *Atomic habits: An easy and proven way to build good habits and break bad ones.* New York: Avery.

Clinton, J., Cairns, K., McLaren, P., & Simpson, S. (2014). *Evaluation of the Victorian Deaf Education Institute Real-Time Captioning Pilot Program 2013: Executive summary.* Commissioned by the Victorian Deaf Education Institute. Melbourne, Australia: Centre for Program Evaluation.

Collins, J. (2001). *Good to great: Why some companies make the leap . . . and others don't.* New York: HarperCollins.

Collins, J. (2005). *Good to great and the social sectors: Why business thinking is not the answer.* New York: HarperCollins.

Comer, J. M. (2019). *The ruthless elimination of hurry.* New York: Penguin Random House.

Covey, S. (1989). *The 7 habits of highly effective people.* Salt Lake City, UT: FranklinCovey.

Danielson, C. (2007). *Enhancing professional practice: A framework for teaching* (2nd ed.). Alexandria, VA: ASCD.

Deci, E. L., & Flaste, R. (2013). *Why we do what we do: Understanding self-motivation.* New York: Penguin Random House.

Deci, E. L., Koestner, R., & Ryan, R. M. (1999, November). A meta-analytic review of experiments examining the effects of extrinsic rewards on intrinsic motivation. *Psychological Bulletin, 125*(6), 627–668.

Deci, E. L., & Ryan, R. M. (2017). *Self-determination theory: Basic psychological needs in motivation, development, and wellness.* New York: Guilford Press.

Department of the Army. (2004). *The U.S. Army leadership field manual: Battle-tested wisdom for leaders in any organization.* New York: McGraw-Hill.

Duhigg, C. (2012). *The power of habit: Why we do what we do in life and business.* New York: Random House.

Dweck, C. (2007). *Mindset: The new psychology of success.* New York: Random House.

Edmondson, A. C. (2019). *The fearless organization: Creating psychological safety in the workplace for learning, innovation, and growth.* Hoboken, NJ: Wiley.

Eisler, R. (1987). *The chalice and the blade: Our history, our future.* New York: HarperCollins.

Erickson, H. L., & Tomlinson, C. A. (2007). *Concept-based curriculum and instruction for the thinking classroom.* Thousand Oaks, CA: Corwin.

Eyal, N., & Hoover, R. (2014). *Hooked: How to build habit-forming products.* New York: Penguin.

Eyal, N., & Li, J. (2019). *Indistractable: How to control your attention and choose your life.* Dallas, TX: BenBella Books.

Fisher, D. B., Frey, N., Quaglia, R. J., Smith, D., & Lande, L. (2018). *Engagement by design: Creating learning environments where students thrive.* Thousand Oaks, CA: Corwin.

Fogg, B. J. (2020). *Tiny habits: The small changes that change everything.* New York: Houghton Mifflin Harcourt.

Frankl, V. (1959). *Man's search for meaning.* Boston: Beacon.

Frazier, R. (2021). *The joy of coaching: Characteristics of effective instructional coaches.* Thousand Oaks, CA: Corwin.

Freire, P. (1970). *Pedagogy of the oppressed.* New York: Bloomsbury.

Fullan, M. (1982). *The new meaning of educational change.* New York: Teachers College Press.

Fullan, M. (2001). *Principals as leaders in a culture of change.* Toronto, Canada: University of Toronto, Ontario Institute for Studies in Education.

Fullan, M. (2008). *The six secrets of change: What the best leaders do to help their organizations survive and thrive.* San Francisco: Jossey-Bass.

Fullan, M., & DuFour, R. (2013). *Cultures built to last: Systemic PLCs at work.* Bloomington, IN: Solution Tree.

Gallup. (2020, December 16). *Measure what matters most for student success.* Gallup Student Poll. Retrieved from www.gallup.com/education/233537/gallup-student-poll.aspx

Gallwey, T. W. (2000). *The inner game of work: Focus, learning, pleasure, and mobility in the workplace.* New York: Random House.

García, H., & Miralles, F. (2016). *Ikigai: The Japanese secret to a long and happy life.* New York: Penguin.

Gawande, A. (2011). *The checklist manifesto: How to get things right.* London: Profile Books.

Gawande, A. (2012, April 16). *How do we heal medicine?* [Video]. TED. Retrieved from www.youtube.com/watch?v=L3QkaS249Bc

Goldsmith, M., & Silvester, S. (2007). *Stakeholder centered coaching: Maximizing your impact as a coach.* Cupertino, CA: THINKaha.

Gonzalez, J. (2015, February 4). Meet the single point rubric [Blog post]. *Cult of Pedagogy.* Retrieved from www.cultofpedagogy.com/single-point-rubric

Grant, A. (2014). *Give and take: Why helping others drives our success.* New York: Penguin.

Grant-Halvorson, H. (2012). *Nine things successful people do differently.* Boston: Harvard Business Review Press.

Grant-Halvorson, H. (2015). *No one understands you and what to do about it.* Boston: Harvard Business Review Press.

Guarino, C. M., Santibañez, L., & Daley, G. A. (2006). Teacher recruitment and retention: A review of the recent empirical literature. *Review of Educational Research, 76*(2), 173–208.

Guba, E. G., & Lincoln, Y. S. (1985). *Naturalistic inquiry.* Thousand Oaks, CA: Sage.

Hall, G. E., & Hord, S. (2019). *Implementing change: Patterns, principles, and potholes.* New York: Pearson.

Harrari, O. (2002). *The leadership secrets of Colin Powell.* New York: McGraw-Hill.

Hatang, S., & Venter, S. (2011). *Mandela by himself: The authorized book of quotations.* Johannesburg, South Africa: Pan Macmillan South Africa.

Hattie, J. (2008). *Visible learning: A synthesis of over 800 meta-analyses relating to achievement.* New York: Routledge.

Hattie, J. (2009). *Visible learning for teachers: Maximizing impact on learning*. New York: Routledge.

Heath, C., & Heath, D. (2007). *Made to stick: Why some ideas survive and others die*. New York: Random House.

Heath, C., & Heath, D. (2010). *Switch: How to change things when change is hard*. New York: Random House.

Heath, C., & Heath, D. (2013). *Decisive: How to make better choices in life and work*. New York: Currency.

Holdengräber, P. (2014). Malcolm Gladwell on criticism, tolerance, and changing your mind [interview]. *Live from the NYPL*. Retrieved from https://www.brainpickings.org/2014/06/24/malcolm-gladwell-nypl-interview/

Holiday, R. (2016). *Ego is the enemy*. New York: Penguin.

Hord, S. M., Roussin, J. L., & Sommers, W. (2000). *Guiding professional learning communities: Inspiration, challenge, surprise, and meaning*. Thousand Oaks, CA: Corwin.

Ingersoll, R. (2006). Understanding supply and demand among mathematics and science teachers. In J. Rhoton & P. Shane (Eds.), *Teaching science in the 21st century* (pp. 197–211). Arlington, VA: National Science Teachers Association.

Ingersoll, R. M., & May, H. (2012). The magnitude, destinations, and determinants of mathematics and science teacher turnover. *Educational Evaluation and Policy Analysis, 34*(4), 435–464.

Johnson, S. (2018). *Farsighted: How we make the decisions that matter the most*. New York: Penguin Random House.

Kagan, M., & Kagan, S. (2009). *Kagan cooperative learning*. San Clemente, CA: Kagan.

Kahneman, D. (2011). *Thinking, fast and slow*. New York: Farrar, Straus & Giroux.

Kahneman, D., & Tversky, A. (1979). Prospect theory: An analysis of decision under risk. *Econometrica, 47*(2), 263–292.

Kirkpatrick Partners. (2009). *The Kirkpatrick model*. Retrieved from www.kirkpatrickpartners.com/Our-Philosophy/The-Kirkpatrick-Model

Klein, G. (2007, September). Performing a project premortem. *Harvard Business Review*. Retrieved from https://hbr.org/2007/09/performing-a-project-premortem

Knight, J. (2002). *Partnership learning fieldbook*. Lawrence, KS: University of Kansas Center for Research on Learning.

Knight, J. (2007). *Instructional coaching: A partnership approach for improving instruction*. Thousand Oaks, CA: Corwin.

Knight, J. (2011). *Unmistakable impact: A partnership approach for dramatically improving instruction*. Thousand Oaks, CA: Corwin.

Knight, J. (2013). *High-impact instruction: A framework for great teaching*. Thousand Oaks, CA: Corwin.

Knight, J. (2014). *Focus on teaching: Using video for high-impact instruction*. Thousand Oaks, CA: Corwin.

Knight, J. (2016). *Better conversations: Coaching ourselves and each other to be more credible, caring, and connected*. Thousand Oaks, CA: Corwin.

Knight, J. (2018). *The impact cycle: What instructional coaches should do to foster powerful improvements in teaching*. Thousand Oaks, CA: Corwin.

Knight, J. (2019, November). A culture of coaching: Why teacher autonomy is central to coaching success. *Educational Leadership, 77*(3), 14–21.

Knight, J., Cornett, J., Skrtic, T., Kennedy, M., Novosel, L., & Mitchell, B. (2010). *Understanding attributes of effective coaches*. Paper presented at the annual meeting of the American Educational Research Association, Denver, CO.

Knight, J., Hoffman, A., Harris, M., & Thomas, S. (2020). *The instructional playbook: The missing link for translating research into practice*. Alexandria, VA: ASCD.

Lefever, L. (2013). *The art of explanation: Making your ideas, products, and services easier to understand*. Hoboken, NJ: Wiley.

Leider, R. (1997). *The power of purpose: Creating meaning in your life and work*. Oakland, CA: Berrett-Koehler.

Lenz, B. K., Bulgren, J. A., & Hudson, P. (1990). Content enhancement: A model for promoting the acquisition of content by individuals with learning disabilities. In T. E. Scruggs & B. L. Y. Wong (Eds.), *Intervention research in learning disabilities* (pp. 122–165). New York: Springer.

Lipton, L., & Wellman, B. (2012). *Got data? Now what? Creating and leading cultures of inquiry.* Bloomington, IN: Solution Tree.

Lopez, S. (2013). *Making hope happen: Create the future you want for yourself and others.* New York: Atria Books.

Lopez, S., & Sidhu, P. (2013). In U.S., newer teachers likely to be engaged at work: Engagement falls about four percentage points after one year at work. *Gallup.* Retrieved from https://news.gallup.com/poll/163745/newer-teachers-likely-engaged-work.aspx

Love, N., Stiles, K. E., Mundry, S., & DiRanna, K. (2008). *The data coach's guide to improving learning for all students.* Thousand Oaks, CA: Corwin.

Malkus, N., & Sparks, D. (2012). Public school teacher autonomy in the classroom across school years 2003–04, 2007–08, and 2011–12. *Stats in Brief. NCES 2015-089.* Washington, DC: National Center for Education Statistics.

Maltz, M. (1989). *Psycho-cybernetics.* New York: Pocket Books.

Marzano, R. (2001). *Designing a new taxonomy of educational objectives.* Thousand Oaks, CA: Sage.

Marzano, R. J. (2017). *The new art and science of teaching: More than 50 new instructional strategies for student success.* Bloomington, IN: Solution Tree.

Marzano, R., Pickering, D., & Pollock, J. (2001). *Classroom instruction that works: Research-based strategies for increasing student achievement.* Alexandria, VA: ASCD.

Miller, D. [@donaldmiller]. (2015, May 5). *The opposite of love is not hate. It's control.* [Tweet]. Twitter. Retrieved from https://twitter.com/donaldmiller/status/595970043915141121?

Miller, W. R., & Rollnick, S. (2013). *Motivational interviewing: Helping people change* (3rd ed.). New York: Guilford Press.

Murphy, K. (2019). *You're not listening: What you're missing and why it matters.* London: Penguin.

Neff, K. (2011). *Self-compassion: The proven power of being kind to yourself.* New York: HarperCollins.

Oord, T. J. (2005, December). The love racket: Defining love and *agape* for the love and science research program. *Zygon, 40*(4), 919–938.

Oxford University Press. (1981). *The compact edition of the Oxford English dictionary.* Oxford, UK: Author.

Pink, D. H. (2009). *Drive: The surprising truth about what motivates us.* New York: Riverhead Books.

Prochaska, J. O., DiClemente, C. C., & Norcross, J. C. (1994). *Changing for good: A revolutionary six-stage program for overcoming bad habits and moving your life positively forward.* New York: HarperCollins.

Quaglia, R. J., & Corso, M. J. (2014). *Student voice: The instrument of change.* Thousand Oaks, CA: Corwin.

Rogers, C. R. (1980). *A way of being.* New York: Houghton Mifflin.

Rosenholtz, S. J. (1989). *Teachers' workplace: The social organization of schools.* New York: Teachers College Press.

Ruiz, M. (1997). *The four agreements: A practical guide to personal freedom.* San Rafael, CA: Amber-Allen.

Ryan, R. M., & Deci, E. L. (2000). Self-determination theory and the facilitation of intrinsic motivation, social development, and well-being. *American Psychologist, 55*(1), 68–78.

Saphier, J., Haley-Speca, M. A., & Gower, R. (2017). *The skillful teacher: Building your teaching skills.* Acton, MA: Research for Better Teaching.

Sattes, B. D., & Walsh, J. (2010). *Leading through quality questioning: Creating capacity, commitment, and community.* Thousand Oaks, CA: Corwin.

Schein, E. (2009). *The corporate culture survival guide* (2nd ed.). Oakland, CA: Berrett-Koehler.

Schein, E. (2013). *Humble inquiry: The gentle art of asking instead of telling.* Oakland, CA: Berrett-Koehler.

Schein, E. H., & Schein, P. A. (2018). *Humble leadership: The power of relationships, openness, and trust.* Oakland, CA: Berrett-Koehler.

Schlechty, P. C. (2011). *Engaging students: The next level of working on the work.* San Francisco: Jossey-Bass.

Scott, S. (2002). *Fierce conversations: Achieving success at work and in life, one conversation at a time.* New York: Berkley.

Seidman, I. (2006). *Interviewing as qualitative research: A guide for researchers in education and the social sciences* (3rd ed.). New York: Teachers College Press.

Seligman, M. E. P. (2011). *Flourish: A visionary new understanding of happiness and well-being.* New York: Free Press.

Senge, P. (1990). *The fifth discipline: The art and practice of the learning organization.* New York: Random House.

Sesno, F. (2017). *Ask more: The power of question to open doors, uncover solutions, and spark change.* New York: AMACOM.

Sinek, S. (2009). *Start with why—How great leaders inspire action* [Video]. TED. Retrieved from www.youtube.com/watch?v=u4ZoJKF_VuA

Smart, G., & Street, R. (2008). *Who: The A method for hiring.* New York: Random House.

Sprick, R. (2009). *CHAMPS: A proactive and positive approach to classroom management.* Eugene, OR: Pacific Northwest Publishing.

Sprick, R., Knight, J., Reinke, W., Skyles, T. M., & Barnes, L. (2006). *Coaching classroom management: Strategies and tools for administrators and coaches.* Eugene, OR: Ancora.

Starr, J. (2016). *The coaching manual: The definitive guide to the process, principles and skills of personal coaching.* Upper Saddle River, NJ: FT Press.

Stevens, D., & Levi, A. (2005). *Introduction to rubrics: An assessment tool to save grading time, convey effective feedback, and promote student learning.* Sterling, VA: Stylus.

Stoltzfus, T. (2008). *Coaching questions: A coach's guide to powerful asking skills.* Virginia Beach, VA: Author.

Turkle, S. (2015). *Reclaiming conversation: The power of talk in a digital age.* New York: Penguin.

Ury, W. (2007). *The power of a positive no: How to say no and still get to yes.* New York: Bantam Dell.

van Nieuwerburgh, C. (2017). *An introduction to coaching skills: A practical guide* (2nd ed.). Thousand Oaks, CA: Sage.

Webb, N. (2002, March 28). *Depth-of-knowledge levels for four content areas* [Unpublished manuscript]. Madison, WI: Wisconsin Center for Educational Research.

Welch, S. (2009). *10-10-10: A life-transforming idea.* London: Simon & Schuster.

Wheatley, M. (2002). *Turning to one another: Simple conversations to restore hope to the future.* Oakland, CA: Berrett-Koehler.

Whitmore, J. (2009). *Coaching for performance: The principles and practice of coaching and leadership* (4th ed.). London: Nicholas Brealey.

Wiggins, G., & McTighe, J. (2005). *Understanding by design.* Alexandria, VA: ASCD.

Wiseman, L., Allen, L., & Foster, E. (2013). *The multiplier effect: Tapping the genius inside our schools.* Thousand Oaks, CA: Corwin.

Wiseman, L., with McKeown, G. (2010). *Multipliers: How the best leaders make everyone smarter.* New York: HarperBusiness.

Wood, W. (2019). *Good habits, bad habits: The science of making positive changes that stick.* New York: Farrar, Straus and Giroux.

Xiao-Mei, Z. (2007). *The secret piano: From Mao's labor camps to Bach's Goldberg Variations.* Las Vegas, NV: AmazonCrossing.

Index

Note: Page references followed by an italicized *f* indicate information contained in figures.

About the Author

Jim Knight, Senior Partner of Instructional Coaching Group (ICG), is also a research associate at the University of Kansas Center for Research on Learning. He has spent more than two decades studying professional learning and instructional coaching. Jim earned his PhD in Education from the University of Kansas and has won several university teaching, innovation, and service awards.

The pioneering work Jim and his colleagues have conducted has led to many innovations that are now central to professional development in schools. Jim wrote the first major article about instructional coaching for *The Journal of Staff Development*, and his book *Instructional Coaching* offered the first extended description of instructional coaching. Jim's book *Focus on Teaching* was the first exploration of how video should be used for professional learning. Recently, Ann Hoffman, Michelle Harris, Sharon Thomas, and Jim introduced the idea of instructional playbooks with their book on that topic.

Jim has written several books in addition to those described above, including *Unmistakable Impact, High-Impact Instruction, Better Conversations*, and *The Impact Cycle*. He has also authored articles on instructional coaching and professional learning in publications such as *Educational Leadership, Principal Leadership, The School Administrator,* and *Kappan*. Through ICG, Knight also conducts coaching workshops, offers courses on the Radical Learners website, hosts the Facebook Live program *Coaching Conversations*, and provides consulting for coaching programs around the world.

He is on Twitter (@jimknight99), Instagram (@jimknight99), and LinkedIn (www.linkedin.com/in/jim-knight-158b6b22).